LET
GO
of the
RING
the hope chapel story

STRAIGHT STREET
PUBLICATIONS
P.O. Box 608 • Kaneohe, Hawaii 96744

LET GO OF THE RING

Copyright ©1993 Ralph Moore

Straight Street Publications
Box 608
Kaneohe, Hawaii 96744

The authors acknowledge use of the *New American Standard Bible*, © The Lockman Foundation.

Moore, Ralph and Dan Beach
LET GO OF THE RING

ISBN O-9628127-1-4
Printed in the United States of America

10 9 8 7 6 5 4 3 2

On a "street called Straight," scales
fell from the eyes of Saul of Tarsus. It
was there that he began to see the way
that led to establishing the Church in
new territories. It is our goal to stir
your thought and increase your vision
for expanding the Church
into all nations.

STRAIGHT STREET
PUBLICATIONS
P.O. Box 608 • Kaneohe, Hawaii 96744

A Word of Thanks

Our rewards in this life reflect our treasures in heaven.

Human relations are the best of His gifts during our earthly walk. This book is not the story of one man, but the faith-journey of thousands of interlocking friendships. Without these people's clear eyed, courageous intent to please God, these events would not have taken place. This story reflects my great privilege in knowing these fine people, sharing life with them.

At the heart of my journey are those closest to me. My patient and trusting wife, Ruby keeps me standing. My children Carl and Kelly stand strong in the Lord and give testimony to God's grace in another generation. These are my rewards.

CONTENTS

Preface

A book like this might seem pretentious.

You may ask, "Why would this man be so bold as to write his own story?"

It's really not my story but that of the Holy Spirit interacting with the several thousand people who make up one small part of the family of God.

This is the story of a family of Christians that begins with Hope Chapel in Hermosa Beach, California and spreads through several generations of new churches in the Western United States and the Pacific Basin. Some use the name Hope Chapel, many do not. It is also the story of the Foursquare denomination and the amazing love within this larger church family. It is love that causes these folks to stretch and flex, enabling the Holy Spirit to work variety into their ranks.

I originally wrote the book for the people of Hermosa Beach in 1983, when I resigned as their pastor. The book was simply an in-house project designed to help them preserve their own church heritage. Over the years others have asked for an update. This book is an attempt to carry the story forward.

There's a lot of "name dropping" in the book. That's intentional. Every life is built upon those that surround it. I think it is important to portray the network God uses in building his kingdom. Some of my friends might not appreciate each other's doctrine or style of ministry. The important thing is that I appreciate them and they all contributed to what has become "the Hope Chapel story."

I pray that the Lord of Glory will use these pages to move you out of your boundaries into a life of faith and excitement.

In His strong love,

Ralph Moore
Kaneohe, Hawaii

1

LET GO OF THE RING

"You'll never let go of the ring, Frodo, they never do."

My friend, Ken, is my dentist. He had me where I couldn't escape, pinned down in that big chair, mouth propped open, his hands deftly working a very long needle into my jaw.

"They never let go when they get to your place. It just isn't done. There is too much pride involved. You'd have to really sell out and I don't think you can."

In J.R.R. Tolkien's splendid trilogy, "The Lord Of The Rings," a hobbit named Frodo (a small, human-like forest creature) is faced with a dilemma. He possesses a ring that can give him control over the whole world. But at the same time it can corrupt the owner and turn him into a despot. If he destroys the ring, a godly order will be restored to the world, but he will be left powerless. If he obtains it, he can rule and take his chances with the moral corruption that accompanies the power of the ring.

You'll have to read *The Lord of the Rings* to find out what Frodo did; this is a story about what happened to me.

I had just told my friend Ken that I felt God calling me
to leave my very secure job of ten years, to start a church
in another city involving people of an entirely different
racial and cultural background.

It meant leaving the pastorate of a congregation of over
two thousand people and a home in a California beach town
that fits like my own skin. I'd be leaving friends that I love
dearly. All this at a time when I was becoming the focus of
incredible attention in the national and local media.

UPI had just put out a story about our church that ran on
radio stations and in newspapers across the country. Now
the TV networks were doing follow-up interviews. We were
even written up in Esquire Magazine. It was pretty heavy
stuff to leave behind for the relative obscurity of a pioneer
pastorate in a distant city where I knew practically no one.

Ken was right. It would be difficult to leave the security
that I knew for the insecurity of a pioneer relocation.
However, he was wrong.

The Bible is loaded with stories of people who have let
go of the "ring" in their lives. The ring, as Ken spoke of it,
represents power, position and prominence. Most important-
ly, it represents control of our lives. All the things we cling
to for security are things that God wants to disrupt. We
must learn to let go of those things, to lay down our life,
pick up our cross and follow Jesus. Christianity works best
in the tension of letting go, so we can receive; of seeking
to lose our life, so we can find it.

God called Abraham to leave his father's house, his
idols, his friends, the familiarity of his circumstances, the
promise of his father's inheritance, as well as the political
power of his wealth.

God told him to get up, leave his father's house and go into a land that He would show him.

The Lord didn't tell Abraham where he was going or what he was going to find. He didn't describe the geography or introduce him to any of the people along the way. He simply said, "Leave this place behind and go into a land that I'll show you." He didn't even give him a map.

But He did promise to bless Abraham if he had the guts to go.

After Abraham left his father's house, God started to define the blessing. God promised that He would give him a son. He promised that He would, through that son, make a nation of people. He promised that, through that nation, all the world would be blessed. He promised that He would go with him and that He would stand with him, that anyone who would bless Abraham, God would bless; and anyone who would curse Abraham, God would curse.

Abraham was called to let go of the ring and trust God, to walk by faith and not by sight. I believe that God calls us all to live that way.

As you move on through the Scripture, you come upon Moses forsaking the riches of Egypt to serve God. You find Daniel, abandoning potential success in the king's house, by eating the way God commanded in the Law. You discover young Jeremiah leaving his occupation, and Amos selling his fig farm to go serve the Lord. Shadrach, Meshach and Abednego not only let go of the ring of power and position in Babylon, they laid their lives on the line when they refused to worship the statue of the king.

In the New Testament, we encounter Jesus at the desk of a wealthy businessman. He looks Matthew straight in the face and says, "Follow Me." There's no definition, no direction. He doesn't promise to make him an apostle. He doesn't tell him he will become a best selling author. He only says, "Follow Me."

Matthew is in jeopardy. Every relationship, everything he possesses, his stature in the community is all up for grabs. Without anything to cling to but trust, he lets go of the ring and he follows after the Lord.

Letting go is hard. But it's the only way to success. As I think back on my life, I've faced the same dilemma as Matthew and Abraham. I've been asked to let go of that ring of control and security. I remember a time when I was seventeen...

2

CHOICES

The crisis came when I was about to enter my senior year of high school, but the dilemma started when I was about six years old.

That occasion was the first time I can remember any direct communication from the Lord and it wasn't very pleasant. I was standing at the top of the staircase where we lived. My two year old brother in the bedroom across the hall let out a horrible scream; my sister must have pinched him.

As my Dad mounted the stairs he told my mother, "With those lungs that kid ought to be a preacher." (This comes on the heels of my father wanting to move us from Portland to Los Angeles in order to go to Bible school so he could preach. I hated the idea. It meant leaving my school, my friends and all that.) The next thing my father said as he came up the stairs was, "Gosh, I wish one of my boys would wind up being a pastor some day."

Something inside of me screamed, "It'll be him not me, I never want to be a preacher!" From that day on I knew (and I can't tell you how I knew, but I knew) God had spoken to me through my Dad. I rebelled inside. As much as a little kid can get angry, I was angry.

For the next thirteen years I fought with the memory of that day. I would never really serve the Lord, because I knew that to let go all the way meant being a preacher, and I wanted to be an architect. I went all through high school rebelling against God's call to pastor.

I went to church, prayed and read the Bible, but lived like the devil at school with my friends. My friends and I went to camp every year and disrupted the place. Once we fed laxatives to a kitten and let it loose in a church service. Another time we cut off the electric power to the dining hall and auditorium when they were washing dishes and getting ready to start church. The pranks went on and on.

At one particular meeting I filled a huge hypodermic syringe with water. During prayer I shot all that water at the ceiling and we had rain. However funny it was, I felt sick at myself for having done it. I told my friend Wendell Cox that I was tired of being a two-faced Christian.

He felt the same way, and we made a decision to end our double-minded life style.

Our plan was to read ten chapters of the Bible a day for thirty days and then to come to a decision. Either we would serve the Lord consistently or get out of church and really taste the "delights of the world," which for two seventeen year old boys mostly meant women.

I read three hundred chapters of the Bible and could not escape the spirit-filled life that came with it. I committed myself to do whatever God asked. The problem was that I already knew what He wanted. He had asked when I was only six.

I was seventeen and faced with a dilemma. If I was really going to follow the Lord, I was going to have to do what He said. But I didn't want to be a pastor, I wanted to be an architect.

I was in a college architectural program at my high school. Buildings that I designed had been built and I felt fairly successful at a very early age. I didn't want to let go of all that. Those things may not seem consequential to you, but at seventeen years old, it was my whole world.

The ring is hard to release. Not only was I faced with the dilemma of changing careers, there were other costs as well. There were my friends, most of whom opposed my decision. The night before I left Portland to go to Bible college in Los Angeles, a friend of mine took me to a restaurant where he spent two hours trying to convince me that I was making a mistake and that it was going to cost our friendship. My employer pulled me aside, telling me that I should go on and pursue a business major and then move on to architecture. He was even willing to help finance my education if I would stay in Portland. My parents weren't sure that I was making the right decision. I remember leaving my girlfriend knowing that my decision would cost me the hope of ever marrying her.

Whatever I had that could please me, in architecture, security, money, influence in the community, all of that had to be passed aside. I had to let go of the ring, lay down my life, take up my cross and follow Jesus.

3

A L.I.F.E. SENTENCE

When I entered L.I.F.E. Bible College in the fall of 1965, I really enjoyed it for the first few weeks. Then I began to cling to the ring.

At first it was exciting to be in Los Angeles. I enjoyed the fast pace, the endless summer, even the city itself. Those were the days when the glory of Los Angeles was just beginning to fade. We were encountering the drug revolution and campus rebellion, but there was still the security of the easy-living fifties and early sixties about which the Beach Boys sang.

Los Angeles was a good place to live. On top of that, it was fun to be in college. We would stage fake fights in the dorms. One time some guys started a fake fight out in the street in front of the school, to upset the neighbor ladies. Another student called the cops on them and we all had a good laugh. There were a lot of other pranks and all the fun that makes college a great experience for a young person.

It was during those days that I met my wife. I had no money, so we became great friends by going for walks in the park or riding the bus to the beach.

It was a good experience in those early days, then frustration set in. I didn't really like the school. The college was small, its recent graduates hadn't really accomplished a great deal, and it had a self-inflicted inferiority complex. The end result was a lot of busy work.

What I considered silly routines and meaningless rituals were forced on us, and class work was anything but challenging. The school certainly did not measure up to my expectations. I knew the history of L.I.F.E. Bible College and the exploits of its early graduates. They stood in stark contrast to the school as I found it.

They even had a dress code. We weren't allowed to wear Levi's or Bermuda shorts. To protest, some of us wore clothes that fit the dress code, but never changed them. One time I went for a whole month wearing the same two shirts on alternating days.

I was very depressed about the whole situation. Teachers would give assignments, but nobody would do their homework on time. Diligent students were penalized by teachers giving extra time when others cried on due day. I started writing notes on the top of my papers in red ink grading the teacher on her performance with the homework before I turned it in.

It became frustrating for me, and I began to wish that I had gone to the University of Oregon or Stanford. I found myself looking for another Bible College to attend, and sent away for catalogs from every school I could find in my first year.

I even remember one day when the dorm manager stopped us from playing catch with a softball because he said that Sunday was the Sabbath. The whole school seemed "Mickey Mouse"to me, but my responses to it were immature. I chaffed against everything around me. God had put me in a situation where He wanted me. He constantly reassured me I was in the right place, but I continued to rebel at my circumstances. Since then I've found that you grow fastest in humbling situations, but at the time I didn't understand, and as a result I sinned by my poor attitude.

Paul writes in Romans 13 that rulers and authorities are established by God. He says we are to submit. As we do, our pride is usually injured. We lose control to the Lord and those in authority over us. Outwardly the situation can look hopeless but God seems to use the peripheral elements of a situation to bless us.

Let me tell you how it worked for me.

L.I.F.E. Bible College was like God's steam iron taking a couple of prideful wrinkles out of my life. Beyond that, the school blessed me in many ways, although I was too immature to notice at the time. During the time I was in school I met and married my wife. I was also fortunate to be tutored by a fantastic educator, Dr. Dorothy Jean Furlong. Any ability I have to teach and maintain a rapport with an audience is a gift of the Holy Spirit bestowed through my association with this tough-minded, yet sensitive and challenging woman.

I became good friends with a man named Jack Hayford who today pastors a congregation called The Church On The Way. Jack had a strong imprint on my life. He was director of the youth program for the Foursquare denomination and his office was near our campus. He befriended and coached me through a lot of my struggles in those years.

There was another very important woman who became a tower in my life. Her name is Eloise Clarno and she works as director of Sunday Schools for the denomination.

She listened endlessly to my complaints and frustrations, always encouraging me to press on and keep on track.

I went to school to get an education, assuming I would get it all in the classroom. I didn't understand that my being in the school afforded relationships with people that God was using to shape me into a pastor.

We were required to attend chapel every Friday, and I hated it. To me, it was just a poor excuse for church, and I was already involved in a great church. However, in one chapel service, we were taught by a man named Barney Northcoat who had pioneered a church about twenty years earlier. It had grown from just a handful of people up to a congregation of 650 people. His story and spark of adventure made a remarkable impression on my life. I sat and listened and felt the adrenaline flow through my body like never before. I listened to this man share his fears and failures as he had built his church.

Something bit me that day; it seemed that God indicated Barney's experience was to be my own. That delighted me. In school I had listened to friends discussing their desires to go out and pastor upon graduation (you have to understand that L.I.F.E. Bible College is basically a"pastor factory"). Classmates would covet this pulpit or another one. Some were already beginning to shine the old apple as they hoped to work their way into some of the larger pulpits of America.

I was angry at all this talk and Barney Northcoat offered a Godly alternative...

4

LEARNING BY DOING

L.I.F.E. Bible College required all students to work in a church as a volunteer, ministering to people. You could teach Sunday School or work with a youth group, even preaching in a convalescent hospital. But whatever it was, you had to get some kind of practical experience. Whatever I might have felt, the overall effect was beneficial to me. It thrust me into the ministry.

I found myself involved in a tiny church in the San Fernando Valley in a place called Granada Hills. Many of the families had just moved away as a result of an industry-wide aerospace layoff, and Art Miller, the new pastor, found himself left with about thirty-five people on his first Sunday.

Art came to the dorm on my first Sunday in the college, trying to recruit my gregarious, talented roommate to work with him. My roommate, Thom Whitaker, turned him down. I felt very embarrassed and untalented as I asked Art if it would be okay if I came to his church. You have to understand that for me to go to this church, he'd have to drive seventy miles round-trip. Seventy miles was a good deal considering Thom, with all his talents, but I was no Thom Whitaker. He said "yes", and I ended up recruiting eight other people. So nine of us crammed into a station wagon each Sunday to help get the church off the ground.

For me, it was almost a pioneer church situation and I was able to learn the ropes of building something out of nothing. We never had enough finances and yet God always met the needs of that congregation.

I learned a fantastic lesson the day the men added a section on the auditorium. They had torn away much of the roof and an outside wall in order to mount a steel I-beam in the structure. The hot August afternoon broke up in a freak thundershower that threatened the exposed interior of the building. Not only would carpeting and furniture be ruined, but electrical junctions would be exposed to water.

Instead of rushing to the roof with yards of plastic tarp, those men got on their knees and prayed. The storms passed us by. There was rain around all sides of the property but none on our lot. I was overwhelmed by their faith and by the Lord's response.

At a youth rally in our church just prior to the end of my freshman year, I met a young guy named Jerry Cook. He had just graduated from Fuller Seminary and had served as youth pastor in the Foursquare church in La Puente, where my wife grew up.

I had a good rapport with Jerry. He was only twenty-five and was headed to pastor a pioneer church located about four miles from my parent's house in a little town called Gresham, Oregon. I accompanied him there. I heard him speak in late May and got all excited about his vision. We arrived in town in the latter part of June, and I was able to attend his first day as pastor.

The congregation had existed for more than ten years. When Jerry arrived along with myself and a couple of friends, the grand total of the congregation was 28. These people had been together for all this time but there had been no real leadership. They met in an ancient wooden church building, with a parsonage next door. Someone had set it on fire and burned most of the roof and second story. The city had condemned the building, but it was still standing. It just stood there looking ugly. The congregation leased the whole property for $1.00 a year. These were demoralized people.

I was fortunate to watch Jerry's mistakes and successes in those first few months. Throughout the summer he preached on the first letter of John and concentrated on the love of God. He taught of God's care for us.

I was able to teach a Sunday School class, made up of people ages 12-36. It wasn't exactly your typical junior-high girl's class. We experienced a tragedy that summer. A young man in that class accidentally blew the back of his head off with a shot gun. He had been playing around and showing off for his friends at the gas station where he worked. He put an empty shot-gun in his mouth and pulled the trigger. The night before the accident someone had loaded the gun. The tragedy was horrifying, but I was learning from Jerry how to handle shocking circumstances.

The denomination put money down on a building that had belonged to the Church of Christ. They believed in Jerry and invested dollars to prove it. About ten weeks into his pastorate, the church had moved.

One day I was out weeding the church yard and God spoke to me. He reinforced what he had said that day in chapel and told me that I had been allowed to work with Art Miller and Jerry Cook because I was going to be a pioneer pastor.

I was frightened, but thrilled with the challenge.

5

STUDENT BODY PRESIDENT

Someone finally called my bluff regarding my stinky attitude towards college. I was receiving a good education both in and out of the classroom, but I was still pretty obnoxious. I was feeling secure enough with things to get pretty loud about my opinions. I began to sound off about policy around the school.

Jack Hayford was now on the faculty both as an instructor and Dean of Students. He was working to improve the faculty, and had plans to build a prayer chapel for the students.

A friend of mine felt that we needed a student center a lot more than we needed a new prayer chapel, since we already had a prayer room on campus. You have to understand that LIFE Bible College is located in Echo Park, a really tough Los Angeles neighborhood.

Off campus, fraternizing was very difficult, and the three-acre campus didn't offer too much space for student activity. We began to lobby and rally for a student center and some vacant classroom space.

I found myself going head to head with other people's feelings. Frankly, I was causing a lot of trouble. One day Jack called me into his office. He told me I was a rabble rouser and pressed me to get more involved in the channels of student government. We had a four- hour talk that afternoon and he made a lot of sense to me. However, at some point I decided I wasn't going to get involved. I would back off and leave everyone alone; let them do their thing and keep my mouth shut.

A few weeks went by and student elections were due. I received a phone call from Jack asking me why I hadn't had courage to run for student office. The school had changed its government and had upgraded the positions of the student body officers and input was now possible.

I shrugged my shoulders and said I wasn't interested. He reminded me that I always had so much to say, and suggested I ought to put my money where my mouth was. I still remember walking to the campus that Saturday morning to fill out the petition to run for Student Body President.

The election came off in a tie. I had run against two of my best friends, and faced an old roommate in the run-off and somehow I won.

I was very surprised. It was the first time that I had ever really gotten involved in school. I'd been hanging on to that ring. You can't stay in control if you take chances with things like elections.

I gave my best. Four of us, Allona Elitmorpe, Dale Downs, Donna Tallent and myself put three hours a day on top of our studies, and worked into our roles in Student Government.

It was one of those sideline educations God had for me. I was still in an institution that I hadn't fully grown to appreciate and yet God was blessing me with another surprise education. My role as Student Body President stretched me and brought me to a place where I learned to motivate and lead large numbers of people. It was something I had never gotten from any classroom experience. These were valuable lessons that cannot be taught in a classroom. As I look back, I only regret that I wasn't open to make better use of all four years in that college. I was simply too prideful and too worried about staying in the driver's seat to make the best of it.

6

GO!

By the time that I was ready to graduate from L.I.F.E. Bible College I was feeling pretty secure, almost cocky. My experience as Student Body President had been a very good one. We had rallied the students to attend social events and ball games to the degree where we had 80% involvement. The Student Body Treasury tripled in one year and we created a Student Body Building Fund for the school that was able to generate $10,000.00 a year. Things generally flourished and it all went to my head.

I changed jobs a lot while I was in college, moving from a part-time job when I had a heavy schedule in the Fall, to a full-time job in the Spring. This way I could make some money and keep myself afloat financially.

In my last quarter I had a pretty cushy part-time job at the Los Angeles Times. I walked into the Personnel Office and asked the director for a job. When he asked me what I could do, I looked him straight in the eye (trembling inside), and told him I could do any part-time job better than anybody else in the place. I wrote out an application including a reference from Brunswick Bowling Corporation where I had earned journeyman carpenter's wages for two summers. This man was very impressed that anybody would pay me that much money at my tender age and I told him about my schedule and refused any jobs interfering with classes or my schedule as Student Body President. By then he was really impressed and began to look for work for me.

The job he came up with was really something. Mostly we did customer relations work, but my position included a strange twist. Every day for an hour and a half I put on a white shirt and tie and delivered newspapers on a little chrome cart. I had an executive newspaper route; I delivered the late final edition to Otis Chandler, Editor in Chief of the Los Angeles Times.I even rode downstairs with him in his private elevator once.   I was pretty impressed with all that went on in the building; the way they operated, the pride that everyone took in their jobs, but more than that I was impressed with myself.

I thought I was hot stuff, rubbing shoulders with those people. It created pride and caused me to try to slip out of the timing the Lord had for my life.

I was going to pioneer churches right then. Although the church in Granada Hills had offered me a very good job with adequate pay upon graduation, I decided to back out and go set the world afire for Jesus at age twenty-two. I was taking the ring back into my hands.

I walked into the pastor's office to turn down the job offer. He was in the midst of a phone conversation and invited me to sit in a big red leather chair until he finished. No sooner had I sat down than this horrible clammy sweat and nausea began to coat my body from my feet upward. I prayed, "Lord, what is going on?" He replied, "You are making a mistake".

On the spot, I decided to stay in Granada Hills and serve the pastor and congregation. The sickness immediately subsided. When Pastor Miller got off the phone and asked me what I came for, I smiled and replied I just wanted to reaffirm my commitment to the job.

Those next three years were some of the best of my life. I matured and learned practical elements of the ministry. But I nearly missed a wonderful opportunity for growth by my pride and impatience. Looking back on the school and my job, I felt ready to take on the world. God stopped me, but He had to use momentary sickness to get my attention. I was still too much in control. My desire to start a church was healthy, even God-given. My timing was lousy and self-generated. The Granada Hills years were fun. God taught me through Art Miller. I made several costly mistakes, often angering people, but Art backed me up and piloted me through often treacherous waters.

The church was healing, healthy and growing. I was able to learn from the congregation's mistakes as well as successes.

Two kids in the youth group really stood out. Dan Boyd was a tall, lanky 12-year-old with braces when we met. By the time I was hired he was 15 and a real clown. Jeff was the pastor's son and I had known him since he was about 8. They were all good kids but Dan and Jeff stood out whenever concern for the Lord would show. Both Dan and Jeff became leaders in the youth group and today both are successful pastors. Their buddies, Bill Vira and Tim Correa, Dan's brother Dudley, and Jeff's brother Rodney were a welcomed backdrop for uproarious jokes and pranks.

When my 15 year old brother-in-law, Tim Correa, moved in with Ruby and I, it was Dan who befriended him and Jeff that got him a job. When Tim accepted the Lord, Dan taught him to live like a Christian.

Under Dan's and Jeff's leadership, many young people came to Christ and a very effective witness went out to the largest high school in the country. They organized a 6:00 a.m. prayer meeting every Tuesday morning with about 30 high schoolers in attendance. They held a Bible study at noon on the campus, singing Jesus songs right next to the radical "Students for a Democratic Society". A couple of SDS leaders were saved as a result.

After two or three years, I was feeling so secure that I didn't want to leave. I brushed aside ever pioneering a church. I read about a 76 year old man in New York state who was a youth director in a very large church and ran a youth meeting with 900 kids every week. I decided that was for me. I was going to do what he did.

I had another day in the pastor's office. I walked in and I made a big announcement that I was going to commit the rest of my life to that job. I was going to stay there and minister until I retired. Even as I said the words I had a sinking feeling inside me that God had other plans. The process of leaving Granada Hills really began before it all had started.

Early in my college days I had taken a bunch of Jr. High school boys from the church to Lunada Bay in Palos Verdes to go snorkeling. On the way home we were driving up Manhattan Beach boulevard toward the freeway. I'm cruising along in my Volkswagen convertible thinking "I'd love to live at the beach. I wonder if our denomination has a church in this town. If so, I want to pastor it." A really covetous, carnal thought.

About half a block later, by the fire station on Manhattan Beach Boulevard, there appeared a little Foursquare church. As I looked at it my first feeling was guilt, "Oh I shouldn't have been praying that way. That's really stupid. How carnal!"

After that day, whenever I remembered that church, I would pray that God would bless the community through that pastor. I prayed that way often, not knowing why.

I didn't know that a man named Carl MacLean had pastored that church faithfully for seven or eight years. He and his son, Jim, had built that building almost by themselves. Just about the time of my coveting session in the car, he died of a heart attack. More than likely, the building killed him. His wife comes here every summer on her vacation and greets me praising the Lord.

Several years later, while living in Granada Hills, and feeling very secure in my job, I received a phone call from a friend of mine named Roy Hicks, Jr. He had just been offered a job as a pastor of a church in Eugene, Oregon. He called me and said, "I want you to come and help me. The church has a duplex, you can have half of it to live in. They pay $90.00 a week. I'll give you $40.00 of it to become Assistant Pastor."

I wanted to go. Roy is a guy I've always loved and respected, a real dear friend. I said, "Well, I'll pray about it". I hung up and got on my knees. I hardly started to pray when I heard what seemed like an audible voice. It was as if someone was standing to my right, just behind me. The voice said, "What if Manhattan Beach opens up and you're in Oregon?" So I got right back on the phone. I told Roy, "I'm not coming, I don't think the Lord wants me there".

He laughed, "You sure prayed fast. It hasn't even been five minutes since I called you." I wasn't about to tell him I thought I heard God talk to me. I just knew he'd think I was crazy. A few months later I shared the story with a friend of mine, Jim Hayford, Jack's brother.

Another year or so later, I went to lunch with Jim who was then the District Youth Director for Foursquare churches. The day before, he had been offered the church in Manhattan Beach. The congregation had called it quits and the plan was for Jim to turn it into a Christian coffee house. He refused. Now, he reminded me, "Hey, do you still want to go there? I remember what you told me a couple of years ago."

I replied sarcastically, "Yeah, I'll go there tomorrow." My wife had just quit her job to give birth to our son, and our family income had just dropped by 70%. We were struggling just to get by, and moving to the beach would mean having no salary at all-just living by faith. That didn't appeal to a certified clinger to the ring like myself.

So, here we were at this restaurant sitting around making jokes about starting a church at the beach. "You could tow banners behind submarines with scripture verses to witness to the skin divers, or you could hire an airplane to tow a 'Jesus Loves You' banner." We were having a smart-aleck's good time when I heard the voice again. Nobody else in the crowded restaurant turned around, so I knew it wasn't audible, but it seemed that way again. Somebody right behind me said, "Go!" The voice was stern and implied, "I don't like your jokes; they're not funny!"

I looked at Jim and said, "You know, maybe we should take this more seriously." I wasn't about to tell him I was hearing a voice. We decided I should go home and tell my wife Ruby. If she was in favor, we would move; if not, we'd stay put. When I got home I was sure that she would say no. Our son Carl was six months old, we'd rented a house for the first time in five years of marriage and I was discussing a job with no guarantee of income.

But she went for it.

The next day we approached the District Supervisor, Dr. Nathaniel Van Cleave. He had been my pastor and professor. He tried to talk us out of going, saying, "I want to send you someplace where there are people already. I don't want to send you to nothing but hardship." I finally had to tell him about the Lord talking to me. His response was, "Oh, so it's that way. Then go, by all means, go!"

7

GOING, GOING, GONE!

The news severely loosened my grip on that old ring.

When we want control, we are coveting God's position in our life. This is the root of sin. Lucifer tried to take God's position and was thrown out of Heaven. Adam and Eve ate the forbidden fruit because it promised the power of choice and would make them "like God". They were thrown out of the Garden of Eden. We grasp for control and want to usurp God's role in our lives. When we do, we are thrown out of His will and His promise of blessing. God doesn't want us to be robots; He does want alert, but trusting people who will obey even in the face of risk. The eleventh chapter of Hebrews details the lives of the faithful, the risk takers, those men and women who consistently surrendered their plans to the Lord.

God expects the same of us. And my move to the beach demanded surrender.

We were guaranteed the use of the Manhattan Beach building plus $150.00 per month to help with overhead. I could take up to 60% per week of the offering, but there were no people to give. The church by that time had been closed for more than four months.

My wife, our baby son and myself, along with my brother-in-law and his friend, moved into an apartment in a run-down section of Redondo Beach in August, 1971. Our rent was $225.00 a month. Our life savings was $2,100. We started church services in mid- September that year.

8

LET GO AND LET GOD

During my years at Granada Hills, Leland Davis was acclaimed a prophet by everyone who knew him. I wasn't so sure. A kind of travelling evangelist, he made the rounds to our church in Granada Hills about once a year. He would interrupt his preaching to prophesy to individuals in the church about very personal things in their lives.

I was troubled by it all. I thought he was a hoax, but couldn't say so because his sister, Ella, was a dear friend of my wife and mine. Then he prophesied to my friend, Ray Boyd, concerning God's blessing in his many business ventures. Every bit of it came true. Leland Davis had my attention.

At a later date, he spoke to me in front of the entire congregation. I was first embarrassed, then frightened as he detailed how I was to fall out of favor with the church and then be restored to a place of respect and fruitful ministry. I'll spare you the details, but that prophesy was fulfilled with painful reality followed by wonderful blessing.

Two weeks before our departure to the beach, Leland came back to Granada Hills. He had another message from the Lord, "The Lord wants you to know that He is going to do a new work through you and through a church that doesn't even exist yet. You are to trust Him and move with the Spirit. It will be different from anything you have seen or can anticipate. It is going to be a brand new thing, you are to relax and trust Him to do it." About a week later, in another situation with no possible knowledge of Leland's words, a lady said almost the same thing. She addressed her words to the whole group, but I felt God was telling me to trust Him and not lean on my own devices.

Over a year later on the first anniversary of "Hope Chapel," we had a guest speaker named Ray Mossholder. After the service, several of us were standing around talking in the back of the auditorium.

Ray suddenly said, "Let's pray." We did until he interrupted with a "word from the Lord." It was as if he quoted what Leland and that woman had said in the San Fernando Valley. There was one difference, he said, "You can't even pray for this, the Lord is going to do something brand new and you can't even visualize it to pray for it." Again, God was saying, "Don't try so hard to control things." He wants us to learn that He knows what He is doing, even when we don't have all the details.

When we relax and trust, we become flexible and more responsive to our calling.

I saw the words "Let Go And Let God!" on a bumper sticker last week. It is a clever, succinct way to summarize everything I'm trying to say in this book, but horribly oversimplified.

God wants us to let go, but that is seldom enough. He wants us to mature, too.

Growth always involves pain. It usually works like this. We let go. Then we encounter difficulties, and freak out. We turn to God, tremble awhile, and finally are rescued by a work of the Spirit. Paul tells us to rejoice about the process. He writes, "We rejoice in our sufferings, knowing that suffering produces perseverance, and character, and a hope that doesn't disappoint, because the love of God has been poured out within our hearts through the Holy Spirit who was given to us.(Romans 5:3)" Let go of the ring, lay down your life and surrender to the Lord. However you say it, there is a price to be paid and a race to be run.

Consider a twenty-five year old preacher with no guaranteed income, in a car with over 154,000 miles on its odometer, driving his wife and infant son around in the heat of August, looking for shelter in the midst of a housing shortage.

Add to that a three-piece suit and a white-wall haircut in a day when everyone was into long hair and ragged clothes. Place the guy in a church building designed for 72 persons with a parking lot built for just seven cars.

Put a vision in his heart for 2,000 people and stand him, suit and all, behind a monstrous pulpit trying to preach to 20 people, including several bikers, a marine corporal, a tiny baby and a topless dancer.

You have a picture of a guy with plenty of trouble to rejoice over. You have a description of me on my third Sunday as pastor of Hope Chapel.

The first week was relatively easy. Only twelve people in the church, all friends. We just sat in a circle and had Bible study.

A friend from Granada Hills named Ron Parks was in the Marine Corps stationed at Camp Pendleton. He brought his mother to play the piano, his sister Susie and her boyfriend Mickie. A little girl, Diane Bennett, from Granada Hills showed up as did Wally and Joyce Larson, who would drive 180 miles a Sunday for 3 months just to help us get started. My own household accounted for the rest. By now a friend named Spencer Morris had moved in, needing a place to stay.

By the third week, I was desperate. Susie had brought a friend, Toni Corbitt, on the second Sunday. We led her to the Lord two days later. Toni proved to be an evangelist, bringing her mother, two sisters, their boyfriends and about ten other people.

Among them were some pretty rough people that I didn't know how to handle.

That third week I went home and cried, "Lord, what am I doing here? I'm not cut out to pastor these people. I'm out of control."

My crisis was triggered when one of Toni's friends, Mike Howard, tried to open a sticky door. I went over to help him. Picture this in your mind: me with my three-piece suit and short hair trying to help this big biker clad in a black leather jacket, engineer boots with steel bottoms and flaming red hair past his shoulders. The door wouldn't open no matter how we shoved. Mike got angry, stepped back, and kicked the door open, while yelling at the top of his voice. I was scared, really scared.

I thought I didn't fit and couldn't do the job. I just wanted to run.

The real problem was my control-oriented, stereotyped view of the ministry. When I finally relaxed, those "rough, long-hairs" turned out to be the backbone of the church. Incidentally, Mike is now a graduate of L.I.F.E. Bible

College and has worked on our pastoral staff. His friend and fellow ex-doper, Randy Wier, used to have a ministry driving up and down Pacific Coast Highway picking up hitchhikers so he could tell them about Jesus. He went on to help pioneer two churches and is about to become pastor of a third. Another of those early converts, John Hille, married one Charlotte Bondt and moved to Houston to start a church.

"Let Go And Let God." It's not all that simple, but it sure works.

In spite of all the traumatic stories of the early years, I dare not forget one wonderful, if quiet person, Mary Deriberprey.

Mary is a soft-spoken Puerto Rican lady now in her 80's and still active in Hope Chapel. She was, in fact, our first member. Before the church was pad-locked, there had been just Mary, the pastor and his wife for several Sundays.

The building had been closed for several months and we had reopened it for about two months before she discovered us. When she came, Mary became one of the pillars of our church. Her age and stability demonstrated that Christianity worked in the long term. That brought hope to our young people. Her letters were a real source of strength and encouragement to me, and I know her prayers stood strong in the face of satanic opposition to the church. Mary is a real treasure.

9

OUR ANCHOR OF HOPE

The name "Hope Chapel" didn't come easily. My wife and I tossed names around for weeks. We bored our friends with a continual flow of church names. It finally came to three choices.

Had we thought to check our phone book, we wouldn't have found, late one nights we drove around South Bay, our three names firmly attached to existing church buildings.

Very depressing!

Our future was pressing upon us. The first service in the "First Church of No Name in the Little Green Building on Manhattan Beach Boulevard" didn't seem real exciting. It was time to lay aside the brainstorms in favor of prayer.

Not to say we didn't pray before, but now we let go of the situation and simply committed it to the Lord.

He came through in one stroke.

One day I was out visiting high school students from the church in Granada Hills, when I felt the Spirit tugging in a new direction. I was leaving a home in Reseda, planning to make my next stop in Newhall, about 20 miles to the north. As I drove to the freeway, my brain kept getting signals to drive to the Valley Book and Bible Store in Van Nuys. It was south and several miles out of my way.

The impressions only grew stronger as I drove into Newhall. So I got off the freeway, turned around, and drove back to Van Nuys. (No, I didn't quickly finish my business in Newhall. If you let go of the ring, you've set to let go completely.)

By the time I got to the store, I was convinced the Lord sent me so He could give me a name for our church.

I felt a little foolish, but I was determined I would walk in the front door, through the aisles, all the way to the back. If something caught my eye, I would investigate. If not, I would go back to Newhall.

The first thing I noticed was a plaque with a crude anchor accompanied by the word "hope." The same symbol appeared on bookends, jewelry, etc. My cynical heart told me that fish and crosses had reached market saturation, so maybe anchors were good for a few more bucks.

I walked to the back of the store and nothing seemed especially noteworthy. I did, however, notice a new book by Francis Schaeffer. As I reached for it, I saw another book describing early Christian symbolism, and thought, "Maybe God sent me here to get a church name out of this book."

Sure enough, there was that anchor with a detailed explanation of its significance.

During the second century of Roman persecution, no one wore crosses on their lapels or Christian bumper stickers on their chariots. Faith in Jesus Christ was only secretly revealed to a trusted friend or neighbor.

One method of revelation was for a person to secretly draw an anchor that looked like our capital letter "J" backwards. If his acquaintance were uninitiated, he would seem to be simply doodling, but if he were a Christian, he would align a "J" symbol to the doodle so that it became an anchor. The anchor was a symbol for Christ, who is the anchor of our souls.

The whole concept is paraphrased by Hebrews 6:19 "This hope we have as an anchor of the soul, a hope both sure and steadfast..."

Early Mediterranean sailors had a trick for overcoming windless days on the ocean. They would load the ship's anchor into a smaller boat and row a few kilometers in the direction of travel. When the line was fully extended, they dropped anchor. At that time, their peers on the ship would winch in the anchor rope, pulling the vessel forward. It was laborious, but it worked.

The smaller boat was called the "forerunner." and it was the anchor that offered way of travel.

Jesus is our hope; He is our anchor.

We picked up the anchor symbol for our logo and called the congregation "Hope Chapel." Our hope being Jesus Himself, who has gone before us as a forerunner and an anchor to assure our arrival in a place He has prepared for us.

Though it was a Biblical name, we took a lot of flack for it. It seems other pastors dealt in faith, not just hope. In ignorance, they threw away the scriptural concept of hope.

The Lord, though, understands hope and hopeless people. He gave us a name that gives a promise of help and a new way of life. Hope is as necessary to the bag lady in the street as it is to the president of a thriving company. Everyone is looking for an anchor.

10

HOW TO BUILD A CHURCH

As Hope Chapel got going, I encountered this old hang-up again. I had enjoyed some pretty exciting times in the ministry in Granada Hills. On a couple of occasions, we had twice as many people at a youth activity as we had in the whole congregation. But for some reason, I felt that the youth group consisted of a meeting of about 30 kids that we held on Sunday evenings. Occasionally the number would swell way beyond that, but it was a group of 30 kids in the long term. As a result, I had this misconception that I was only capable of pastoring about 30 people. I really lost sleep over this hang-up.

When we started the church we had fewer than 30 people for several weeks. There would be 22 people or 24 or 28, then 21 people again but never over 30. I was really frustrated and began to seek the Lord. During those days I hung on to those prophecies about God doing a new thing. I guess fear was a blessing, because it drove me to serve the Lord.

God indeed did a new work, but it came in some unexpected ways. One of those was a conference that I attended at Crystal Cathedral in Garden Grove. I heard Robert Schuller talk and was pretty impressed with the man. I had already read his book, *Move Ahead With Possibility Thinking.* In the book he told of his own fears, frustration and his intent to believe God, to seek the Lord, and grow in faith, which he calls "possibility thinking." Over and over in that seminar I heard the statement, "With men it's impossible, but with God, all things are possible." He also said, "If there is something you think God has called you to do and if there is any way you can envision accomplishing it, then it probably wasn't God, because God will only call you to do things that are bigger than you are. Bigger than your resources."

Here I was being frustrated. I thought that I couldn't pastor more than about 30 people, and yet felt that God had called me to pastor a church of about 2,000 people. I even felt the Lord had shown me a building we were to buy that would house a congregation of that size. Schuller's words were a challenge to a greater faith.

Dr. Schuller told how he had found himself stuck off out to the side of a highway as he was driving to California to start Crystal Cathedral. He had $500 in his pocket and an organ on a little trailer. He had gotten a good start and was halfway across the country when a rear tire on his car went flat. He pulled off the side of the road only to discover that his tire jack didn't work. There was no way to change the tire. Faced with this problem, he began to pray, asking God what to do. The Lord directed him to dig a hole underneath the tire with the tire iron. He dug deep enough to get the old tire off and put the new one on. It was a great illustration on how the Lord will show us a way to get through any obstacle that stands in the way of ministry.

The conference taught us to "Find a need and fill it," to look for people who are hurting and find a way to minister. When you look for need, you're often forced to unique solutions. But the Lord is creative and if you seek Him, He gives wisdom. Schuller taught me to trust God and walk the unpaved road, the way that's untried, a way that nobody has gone before. I took courage and confidence from the things that he said.

We looked around our community and found that there were several obvious needs. One was locked up in the narcotic revolution. Everybody under 30 seemed to be experimenting with drugs. The churches were upset, but not reaching out. We cared, but had no resources. In those days if you didn't dress like everybody else, you weren't welcome in church. People using drugs weren't putting on white shirts and ties to come to church.

Another need in our community was for a church that could minister to single adults. If, you weren't in high school or college and you weren't married, the church didn't know what to do with you. It was worse if you were divorced. If you were single for any reason and had a child, you could forget the church. No one else wanted to deal with these people, so we chose to get involved. We decided to cut as narrow a slice of the sociological pie as we could and do the best job possible with these people. We found a need and set out to fill it. We ran ads in the paper and distributed literature targeted at young single adults, particularly those who had been associated with the drug culture.

You can imagine what happened. Many churches in the South Bay reacted against us. We were "just a hippie church" and I was a "slick young kid that wasn't interested in meeting the needs of whole families."

I was involved with families. I wanted to help create them. I had actually prayed that God would turn our church into a "mating ground" for young Christian adults. I watched so many people grow up in church, then become discouraged and finally wander into a bar looking for a mate. They'd get picked up and I'd watch their life go down the drain.

I began to earnestly pray that God would send young single adults into our fellowship, and that as they met there, we could perform some Christian marriages. Hope Chapel was built on the answer to that prayer and is a fairly strong family church, although more than half of our congregation are singles to this day.

Just before starting the church, at a Foursquare pastors' meeting I heard a man speak there who overwhelmed me. He too, was ministering to young single adults. A lot of them were hippies that had flocked into Orange County in those days. Instead of some young guy with a beard and long hair, here was a middle-aged man with a bald head and gray hair, wearing a tan suit and a black turtleneck sweater. Before he spoke, he stood and smiled at us. That smile was about half a mile wide. I'd never seen such a warm, loving smile in my whole life.

His name was Chuck Smith, and his church was Calvary Chapel. He told how God had broken him and released him from the ministry, then brought him back by way of a home Bible study to pastor a small congregation in the Newport Beach area.

He had been intrigued by all the young people turning to drugs and he wanted to meet a hippie. He said he invited a guy to his home who was living on the road, hitchhiking down Pacific Coast Highway from Canada to Mexico, witnessing to whoever would give him a ride. Greatly impressed, Chuck hired him as their youth pastor. The church supplied a two bedroom house for the guy; within a couple of weeks there were 40 people living in that house and yard. God had exploded this ministry into significance.

I was intrigued with Chuck Smith. More than being impressed with him, I was thrilled with some things he had to say. He taught us to cope with the growth by shifting around the church program. I was used to the traditional church, with a full scale Sunday School and then church afterwards. That program demands facilities and a big management team. We had neither. Our church was built to house 72 people. We only had 30, but we were looking toward 2,000.

Chuck said that they had done away with adult Sunday School. He just taught the Bible to adults in church during the same hour as the Kids' Sunday School. That met our need. Chuck got into the scripture and challenged us, through Jesus' statements to Peter. Jesus told Peter that He would be responsible for building His church, and the gates of hell would not prevail against it.

Up to this time, I'd spent my whole life trying to figure out how to build a church. I'd gone to seminars every year where they would have a new plan. It took years for me to discover the reason for the grand new plans was that the old ones never worked. All of us suckers kept paying good money for seminars that taught lousy game plans.

Here, Chuck Smith was quoting Jesus, and Jesus wasn't telling Peter (or me) to build a church. He was saying that He would build His church and that the gates of hell would not prevail against it. That turned me on. He reminded us that Jesus told Peter it was his job to feed the sheep. He said, "If you love me, feed my sheep." Most pastors I knew put "sheep feeding" very low on their priority list. I was one of them. II Chronicles 15 makes a big deal about how lousy things went in Judah without a teaching prophet.

Too often the church lacks a teaching prophet and the people are like starving sheep. Chuck said his mandate as a pastor was to tend the lambs and feed the sheep, and that meant to serve God's Word in generous helpings. It was Jesus' job to build His church.

At that time, Calvary Chapel was the fastest growing, and soon to be the largest, church in North America.

Chuck didn't have any secrets, other than doing what the Lord had said, and anyone could obey the Lord if he chose.

Robert Schuller said, "Find a need," and pointed me toward single adults. Chuck Smith said, "Feed the flock," and role modeled Bible teaching, verse by verse, whole chapters at a time. We couldn't help but be successful.

Life was not free from discouragement. I remember one middle-aged couple who came during the first four months. They took my wife and I out to dinner a couple of times, even brought flowers to my wife. We felt they were our friends. One day she called me crying and saying she wasn't coming to church anymore. The teaching was shallow. It just didn't meet her needs. I really felt bad. I hung up the telephone in despair. We'd gone past 30, but I was hurting that my teaching wasn't up to par.

While I was praying and agonizing before the Lord, the same lady called and took me off the hook. Now she was angry. "Well, I just had to tell you one more thing about the church, and maybe this is the real reason we're not going there. Would those people dress that way if Jesus came to that church?" Click!

I realized that this lady wasn't going to have her needs met anywhere. She was focusing on outward appearances, not new hearts. Jesus was coming to our church and He was saving "long-hairs" who came to the church barefoot and dirty. Jesus was there and he was radically changing hopeless, wrecked lives. I came under other pressures to be a little more "middle-of-the-road", and especially to lay off the singles focus. The old ring made a surprise appearance as the pressure came from our biggest contributors. That one lady, however, catalyzed my decision. I chose to pastor hurting people, as Jesus had said, "It is the sick who need a physician."

11

THE CROSS AND
THE SWITCHBLADE

In our first year, we gave away 20,000 copies of David Wilkerson's book, *The Cross and the Switchblade*, in an attempt to let people know that God cared. Wilkerson was an Assembly of God pastor in a small Pennsylvania mountain town. God called him to New York to witness to five young men on trial for beating a quadriplegic to death in his wheelchair. Unable to contact the men, Wilkerson charged into the courtroom, but was hurled out by the bailiff, making headlines in the New York Times. He never did see the young men he had gone to visit, but the kids in the ghettos saw him as their friend. A prominent gang leader was saved after threatening to kill Wilkerson and a ministry called Teen Challenge was formed.

We didn't have a gang problem, but drugs were every-where. The book would be a perfect giveaway for our location. I contacted a Christian philanthropist, named W. Clement Stone, who had given Wilkerson money to start Teen Challenge and was a friend of Robert Schuller's. We could get the books for 25 cents each so we wrote Mr. Stone asking for $5,000 to buy 20,000 of the books. (There were only 20 of us in the church at the time when I wrote the letter. That meant distributing 1,000 books each.) Mr. Stone gave us the money. We bought the books and attached a little red sticker that read, "Need help? Call Hope Chapel," offering my home telephone number as a 24-hour hot line.

By the time we got the books, we were 6 months into the church and there were 100 of us. That meant we only had to give away 200 books apiece. Still, 20,000 copies of a small paperback book will fill a large trailer house almost to capacity. Eight people worked a whole day just attaching the labels.

Although we'd been given the books, which could retail for $20,000, we did have to buy the labels which cost $72. Our finances were so tight in those days that I wrote a hot check on Friday afternoon and prayed that Sunday's offering would cover it. It did.

In three weeks, the books were gone. Those weeks were some of the most exciting in the history of our church. Churches often come asking people for help. We were offering to help others. When you handed someone a paperback book, he thought you'd given him a dollar. It was nice. People who wouldn't talk about the Lord took time to read the book. We gave them to people everywhere. A group of us smothered a mile of beach on a Saturday afternoon, giving books to everyone we met. I'd even stand outside of junior high schools at 3 o'clock and catch kids on their way home.

Incidentally, just the other day when I was telling this story twelve years later, a very lovely young woman walked up to me. She was new to our church and said, "You know, I remember you coming to my junior high in Manhattan Beach and giving away those books. I visited the church a few times, but I've just now become a Christian. I came back here because of those books."

We went to hospitals because we knew that those people had time to read them. We all handed them out to our friends.

John Hille walked into Hawthorne City Jail with a box of books asking, "Who's in charge of drugs here?" The sergeant bolted out of his chair like he thought the box was full of marijuana. John explained what he had, and the guy replied, "I've got the keys to the jail, let's go." The two of them gave away 75 books to people in that jail.

The plan worked. People came to the Lord. We counseled hundreds of people over the phone and many times the Lord delivered people on hard drugs in an instant when they'd been unsuccessful in long-term drug programs. The neat thing was that we cast ourselves in a servant's role that would result in long-lasting ministry.

One funny little sideline to all this came in the form of people who'd use the hot line number to play pranks on me. Countless Saturday nights were marked by someone calling up to be silly with the sound of a party in the background. Pranks are to be expected, but I sure lost a lot of sleep. It was all worth it, especially when some of the pranksters accepted the Lord and joined our fellowship.

12

WAVES OF FAITH

Finances were very tight during the first six months. My salary one awful week came to fifteen dollars. By comparison, the minimum wage was over a hundred and I had earned four hundred a week as an eighteen year old carpenter.

Finances got tighter when my wife discovered she was pregnant and we were about to become the parents of a beautiful baby girl. God had used the birth of our son, Carl, to put us in a tight spot and He used the arrival of Kelly to keep us there. No way was my wife going back to work now.

We had very little to spend on advertising, so we created a literature piece called "Waves of Faith". It was a bright green, legal-sized page printed on both sides with testimonies of people in Hope Chapel. Best of all, it cost only about twenty-four dollars per thousand. Then I would put on my tennis shoes and run through the neighborhood leaving literature on every door. I could hit 125 houses an hour for a four hour stretch. I lost a little weight, but it was cheaper than paying postage.

For every thousand pieces I put out, a family would join our church. It paid off. Twelve years have gone by, and I'm still in contact with most of the people who came directly or indirectly through that effort. Among them, David Benefiel, Barry Felis, Randy Boldt, Steven Steffe, Greg Frazer, Dale Yancy, and Bobby Chance, have gone on to pastoral ministry.

I was leaving literature at one door, and a lady opened it. I handed her the literature, and she said, "Oh, my daughter might be interested in this." Her daughter, Sue, was dating the leader of a Christian rock band called "Children of the Light". I'd been trying to hire the group to play at our church, but I didn't know how to contact them. Sue came to Hope bringing her boyfriend and his partners. I was still struggling to contact the band when someone said, "They all go to your church." The guys were all wondering why we hadn't asked them to play.

Two thousand houses a week was a nice literature goal, but it couldn't last forever.

The Bible says that it is the job of pastors and other leaders in the church to build up or equip saints (everyone else) to do the work of ministry. The pastor who tries to do all the work will have all the power, but the church will remain stunted.

God taught us a philosophy. All that a pastor does is to be directed toward helping Christians minister, instead of the pastor doing it all. This works kind of like the army. Soldiers fight the war, not generals. It is the generals' job to train and equip the soldiers.

Pop gospel singer Andrae Crouch gave us an opportunity to test our new strategy. I had gone to college with Andrae Crouch, but barely knew him. He was only in the school for two years before his ministry flourished and he left. Several years later, a friend named Glenn Rudy invited me to an Andrae Crouch concert at Melodyland church I was sitting there feeling sorry for myself. I was pastor of such a small church (only 3 months old) and we could never afford to host someone like Andrae. I griped to the Lord throughout the whole evening. Late that night, Glenn called. He had scheduled a dinner meeting with Andrae to discuss a big South Bay concert. He wondered, "Is it alright to bring Andrae to church after the dinner?"

We only told the people in our church. We didn't go on the radio or in the newspaper. This was a special opportunity for our people to invite friends they had been sharing Christ with to the meeting. There were about 40 in the church, and they could invite only their friends. One hundred and twenty-five people showed up. The building was crowded to overflowing. God taught us to use an event or our literature or whatever, to support the saints in their outreach.

About this same time my wife was selling Avon products to keep us in groceries. She managed to get the route that included the church building and about two hundred homes and apartments. We delivered every piece of literature we had to those homes. People knew about us through the literature and were that much more willing to listen to her. The literature supported her witness when she talked to those women face to face and several of those people found their way into our fellowship.

We stopped trying to use the literature to bring people to the Lord. Rather we began to see it as a plow that breaks the soil so that someone could sow face to face.

13

THE SONSHINE INN

The whole idea of reinforcing the saints produced a brand new tradition in Hope Chapel. Our first Thanksgiving we noticed many of our people were far away from their families. Several had left homes in the North or East to live the "good life" in California. Many more people had lived on the road and in very strange locations before they became Christians. During the early seventies a lot of people lived in parks or under the Manhattan Beach Pier. These folks came to our church and got saved. We couldn't leave them alone or in the cold for Thanksgiving, so we turned the whole church into a big dining hall.

One pew sat up against a folding wall, about ten feet behind the next one leaving an aisle space in between. We set a ping-pong table in the aisle. Some sat on the pew and others sat in chairs on three sides of the table. Card tables went into the youth room, and our small office provided a serving area. We had our Thanksgiving potluck dinner on Sunday night. That way we had the benefit of the holiday and our church became an extended family.

Later we discovered this was the exact motivation of the love feasts practiced in the early church. An opportunity for those who had, to share with those who didn't.

Years later, we planned our current building with a small kitchen so we would never be able to have banquets. If our church is to eat together, it has to be a potluck. We call them Love Feasts and schedule them several times a year.

Another lesson in supporting ministry was called the "Sonshine Inn." A couple of guys in the church asked if they could start a Christian coffee house.

Those were the days of long hair and revolutions, and everyone was into coffee houses. Christians were real good at finding old houses and opening them up as a place where forty or fifty young people could sit on the floor and listen to music. Although they were called coffee houses, very little coffee was served. This crowd was into soft drinks.

We couldn't afford to rent a house so we screened off the overflow room at the rear of our auditorium. The kids went nuts. They put posters all over the walls and glued carpet scraps together in a patchwork floor cover. They put together a rock band of four or five regulars with musical instruments and called it "The Sonshine Inn."

We thought it would involve ten or fifteen kids on Saturday night. But they often had a bigger crowd on Saturdays than we did on Sunday mornings for church.

God taught us some things about ministry. First, we found out what could happen if we let it. Too many pastors and elders hang onto that old ring at this point. When you retain close control you hamper the Holy Spirit in the lives of others.

We had let half a dozen new Christians run with the ball and substantial ministry resulted. It was beyond anyone's wildest expectations.

Second, the Sonshine Inn was a focal point for evangelism by young Christians. A person might share Christ well, but not have the courage to invite his friend to pray and ask the Lord into his life. The coffee house supplemented this process and became a harvest center.

It was important that non-saved persons come by invitation rather than by advertisement as the Sonshine Inn was only designed to complement ministry, not perform it.

Some people were regulars on Saturday but never showed up on Sunday due to job schedules. This taught us to provide multiple services to further serve our people.

Another nice lesson was that people, not property, make a church. Every Sunday we lived with an auditorium that looked like a church in the front and a garage in the rear. Some people were a little uptight about it. That forced us to set priorities, and people won over facilities.

14

FOAM RIDER

Every society has its folk heroes. Hope Chapel is no different. I to tell the story of "Foam Rider" (his surfing friends named him that) because he epitomized the first four years of Hope Chapel.

It all starts with Mike Howard (the biker who kicked the door open in our third Sunday). Mike asked for prayer in every service. "Pray that I find my friend Rick. I think he's in jail, but I want to tell him about the Lord."

Pretty soon it became, "Praise the Lord, I found Rick! He just got out of jail for dealing. Pray that I can witness to Him." Then, " Pray for Rick. He nearly beat me up for nagging at him about the Lord."

One Wednesday night a couple of us were standing out side the building teasing a guy named John about his haircut: he had whacked off his shoulder length-hair and shaved his beard. What a shock!

In the midst of this, two bikes came roaring up. One guy is Mike and the other is a guy we didn't know. He had hair down his back and a "Fu Man Chu" moustache, wore motorcycle boots and a new Levi jacket spotted with

bleach, and was driving a chop Harley with flames painted
all over.

They parked the bike and rushed inside. As they passed
us Mike said, "Hi you guys, this is Rick."

To get in the building they had to pass Will Heinle. Will
was an engineer at McDonnell Douglas Corporation and
later became our first associate pastor. He was fifty-eight
years old, bald on top with a close cropped fringe of white
hair all around and wore a Polyester sport coat and tie.
Hardly a close match for two bikers.

Will had this habit when introduced of saying, "Hiya
man," grabbing your hand as if to shake it, then embracing
you in a bear hug. Love just oozed from the man.

He caught Rick Fulenwider at the door on the way in.

The meeting was small-six people. We were sharing
testimonies when Rick spoke up: "I want to share something. Right here, right now I accepted Jesus Christ into my
heart like Mike's been telling me. I've been mad at Mike for
bugging me about the Lord and I came here tonight to start
a fight so he'd get off my back, but," he now pointed at
Will, "that old man over there (sob, sob), he (sob, sob)
hugged me..."

God's love didn't seem to know any "generation gap."

Rick Fulenwider helped me move into our new house the
next weekend. My neighbors told me they were scared that
he was moving in, not me.

The man was rough. One day we went surfing in Venice.
Yes, Rick was a biker who was also a contest surfer with
trophies to prove it. Everyone we met was scared of him.
People would stop talking when he approached. They
showed him great respect.

One guy told us he was going to steal some trunks out of the bag laying by the strand wall. Rick says, "God doesn't want you to do that."

The guy shoots back, "God doesn't want me to steal? What about the guy who's head you busted when he caught you stealing his surfboard?"

Rick: "I said God doesn't want you to steal those trunks."

The guy: "What did you get, religion?"

Rick (jaw tightening): "No, I'm a Christian and God doesn't want you to take those trunks."

The guy: "Oh, you're a Jesus freak!"

Rick is hot now, and He grabs the guy and repeats "No, I'm a Christian..." The guy backed down.

Rick was so rough, yet one day he came to church crying. He had punched some guy while they were surfing and then tried to apologize and witness to him.

He used to "prophesy" in church. Just before I'd preach he'd stand up with a real imposing voice and tell everyone, "That little skinny guy in the suit is our preacher and God talks through him, so you better listen-especially you new people."

The rough edges began to smooth out. One day he told me how he wanted to marry a godly woman.

Another time he testified how five guys in an old car knocked him and a friend off his bike at a red light. He pulled the lock chain off and went after them. "I was going to cut the leader's head in two with that chain until the Holy Spirit stopped me...." He put the chain back on the bike, walked up and told this big guy that Jesus loved him. They all ran away.

Rick had poor teeth all his life. He had saved for months to replace them. The old teeth were removed and we all got to tease him about going toothless.

Then, no Rick.

He dropped out of sight and I started looking for him. A friend told me he was real sick from not eating because he didn't have any teeth. I knew he had the money for the new teeth and that they were long overdue.

It turned out that he gave away the money he had saved to a Christian woman who was hurting worse than he. She was about to lose her house so he gave her the dentistry money. Talk about "find a need and fill it!"

The church council spent benevolence funds on those teeth. It was a great investment.

The Lord answered Rick's prayer about a godly wife, too.

I'll never forget the night Tay Rainey stormed in. "Who is this Rick kid? He says he's going to marry my Nancy!" He no sooner calmed down than I had an upset Rick on my hands. I sent them to talk it out in the parking lot.

Half an hour later, Tay comes back in grinning from ear to ear. "That young man submitted to me. He told me he wants to marry Nancy, but only if I say so. He trusts God to speak through me...." When I asked how he responded, Tay got all weepy-eyed and whispered, "Of course it's all right."

There's more, but the point is that God changed Rick. Today he and Nancy have two lovely children; they own a home and twice have helped others start churches.

Got time for one last "Rick story"? My friend Mike Faye was dating a girl named Cheryl Smalley. I hardly knew either of them at the time, but had prayed with Cheryl when she turned to the Lord. Mike wasn't yet a Christian and he was a little skeptical of all that was going on. Especially at this Hope Chapel Love Feast! He barely got in the door when a biker named Rick gave Mike, the successful businessman, an enormous bear hug. Two days later, through tears, Mike asked the Lord into his heart. He said it was Rick's show of love that opened him up.

Jesus loved Will Heinle. Will passed it on to Rick, and Rick handed it off to Mike. That's evangelism in shoe leather.

15

LOVE AND UNITY

A new church has unique problems. One of which is a tendency for everyone to superimpose their background on the rest of the congregation.

Most of our people were "off-the-street" types, brand new to the church scene. But there were several with a history in other churches. I found myself struggling with disunity in a very small church. Cliques/Groups formed, and each had its own little set of "power-plays" designed to corral me into somebody else's style.

They were all wonderful people with good intent and a solid background that they wanted to duplicate at Hope.

We had a group of people from Calvary Chapel. Another cluster came to us from Church on the Way in Van Nuys. Jack and Chuck both had a big influence on my life. While I was open to the way they did things, I couldn't substitute either man for the Holy Spirit.

Another contingency arrived from Melodyland. The scene rounded out with a solid group of Christians who were bikers and they had grown up under the influence of other members. They had learned to trust the Lord and do as best they could without a lot of formal teaching, but they weren't incredibly solid.

I was pulled in all four directions.

I was teaching from the first chapter of First Corinthians where Paul addresses the same problem. One group says, "We are of Paul"; another declares," We are of Apollos"; still another claims Cephas. The rest claimed they were of Jesus.

The importance is that the whole Church centers on Jesus rather than any man or ministry. Hope Chapel, in particular, had a word from the Lord.

I began to relate to leaders and did whatever I could to equip them. In one day I could easily telephone everybody in any leadership capacity, so communication was simple. We encouraged the variety among ourselves and yet we demanded love and unity around the Lord.

I had to constantly remind myself that the Lord mattered, not Ralph Moore. The temptation was always to grab that ring of power, to control everything. I just maintained a love for, and a relationship with these leaders as long as they were willing to submit to the basic direction of the Church and give in to the principles of oneness that we experienced.

We became an invading army. All platoons united with a common purpose and identity, yet each was unique in approach. In a matter of weeks, we were touching over 200 people a week, and Bible studies spread all over South Bay. We were in factories, hospitals, offices and schools. Some groups centered on prayer, others on didactic Bible study while others majored in gifts of the Spirit. We all came together on Sunday to celebrate mutual victory. I was teaching in several homes and hospital cafeterias, as well as on the lawn at U.C.L.A. Campus next to Bruin Walk.
Once, I was attacked crossing a union picket line to teach out of the book Philippians at a missile factory. God thoroughly blessed these little bands of Christians at a time when many churches viewed home studies as "a tool of the devil." The studies not only brought growth in individuals and the number of people we could shepherd, they gave the leaders a laboratory to develop pastoral skills. They got to operate while in embryo form. In a small Bible study there wasn't too great of a risk of failure, so they could try anything. Several of those men now pastor churches of several hundred people.

Bulletin cover picturing the original church building constructed for sixty people (1971).

Hope Chapel in Manhattan Beach. The original congregation could fit in a Volkswagen (1971).

A "70's style" wedding at dawn on a Sunday morning (1974).

Typical beach baptism. Will Heinle is at far right wearing a wet suit (1974).

Hope Chapel Hermosa participants in "Hawaii Summer Outreach," a street evangelism program sponsored by Kaimuki Christian Church and Pastor Harold Gallagher (1975).

Moore family at Christmas (1975).

Hope Chapel staff 1982.
L-R top row: Don Stewart, Dan Boyd, Zac Nazarian.
Bottom row: Dan Beach, Ralph Moore, Dale Yancy, Randy
Sanford.

Pastor Ralph preaching in the newly refurbished bowling
alley turned into a church (1976).

Pioneer church meeting in a home. Hope Chapel Kihei (1979).

Hope Chapel Kihei Maui and communion on the beach. Craig Englert is in center, Pat Hammon on extreme right (1979).

16

A NEW THING

We never forgot those prophecies the Lord gave us. He had promised He was going to do something that we couldn't anticipate. We used to wonder; we would anticipate anticipating. We'd question what in the world could the Lord be doing that we hadn't seen. Solomon said there is nothing new under the sun, everything has been done once. Really, He wasn't doing anything new at all. It was simply something so old that everyone had forgotten it.

Our church was to mother new churches. It had been a long time since anyone in our circles had sent pastors out to start new churches, especially lay pastors.

The New Testament is an adventure story. A great king, rejected by his people and resurrected after his murder, sends emissaries to the whole world to tell of his life. These men spread the news and plant cells of believers throughout the world in less than a generation. They were very exciting and success-oriented.

Their strategy bears analysis. A dozen men with a world to conquer. All but one of them was executed and the lone exception was imprisoned for life; yet they succeeded.

How? The key was trust, both in God and men.

Wherever they went, they preached to whoever would listen and they had been instructed to brush off those who wouldn't. Among those who listened and believed they appointed leaders to watch over the rest.

The apostles spent as little as three months in a single location. That meant men without formal education caught enough of Jesus to shepherd the flock in so little time. But it worked!

Today, even with our multi-million dollar investments, our billions in real estate and our well-defined Christian establishment, we still long for the success of those early believers.

It seems we've put too much trust in the institution and not enough in the Holy Spirit.

In the 1930's a church called Angelus Temple in the Echo Park area of Los Angeles sent hundreds of men and women all over the world to preach the Gospel and establish churches. These people were scantily trained. First came a three month program, then a three or four year program that invested heavily in an understanding of ministry, and didn't care that much for scholastics.

Churches sprung up overnight and God did His heroics through vessels of clay.

As time went on, institutionalism crept into the Foursquare movement along with the rest of the Evangelical church. Everyone was in a holding pattern. The denomination was expected to pioneer ministry through its headquarters while the local church complained that not enough was happening.

Whatever happened to Acts, chapter 13, where the Holy Spirit interrupted a local church prayer meeting to say, "Set apart for me Barnabas and Saul for the work to which I have called them?" The denominations not the spirit were expected to call, and everyone thought the seminaries provided the only acceptable training ground.

We had discovered the Lord's "new (old) work" almost by accident.

He was right about, "don't pray for it; you can't even anticipate it." Nothing in my background had ever challenged me to think of people in my congregation as the means to launching churches. In fact when we did it, other pastors complained that we were somehow in rebellion to our denomination, even though we had the support of the leadership.

17

BRANCH OF HOPE

Rich Agozino is a daredevil. As a young man he rode all over the United States on freight trains, worked as a seaman, and on a hot tip invested all his savings in gold stocks. During a market roller coaster in 1968, he earned enough money to buy a house.

He was radical; he did everything with all of his heart and might, even drugs. Then he came to Jesus. The guy was so nuts that he hung a sign in the back window of his V.W. van saying, "I'm a fool for Christ, who's fool are you?" Rich was so turned on to the Lord that he was in church or teaching Bible studies every night of the week. His family could hardly keep up with him.

He came into our church by storm. He was teaching a Bible study that was looking for a home. They had out-grown several houses and moved into a church. But they spoke in tongues, and the other church wasn't too interested in having them around. Some of his people had scouted our church and felt that it would be a good place for the Bible study as well as a church home. Rich and I met on a Wednesday afternoon. He put me on the hot seat with about a hundred questions about my past and what we believed.

When I finally passed muster, he decided this would be his church home.

He and I became very close friends. Rich was preparing to go to New Zealand as a missionary.He was teaching Bible studies four nights a week, in addition to a full time job as a finish carpenter plus his role as husband and parent. The straw that broke the carpenter's back was a fifth study group.

A number of young families were missing Sunday evening service due to the difficulty of getting their little kids to bed late and driving quite a distance to church. We sent church to them. Rich Agozino held Sunday night church in a home in Torrance while the rest of us met in Manhattan Beach.

The preparation and teaching load was getting him down. Sometimes God has to put a person in a tight spot to get his attention.

Preparation for New Zealand was still underway when the two of us heard Don MacGregor talk about church growth. Don had been one of two American missionaries to the Philippines from our denomination. Under his leadership, a house church/lay pastor movement spawned as many as 55,000 converts a year. These people were living the Book of Acts.

Don spoke every night for a week, but it took only about fifteen minutes for Agozino and me to decide his immediate future. New Zealand was out.

We heard Don in early October, 1973 and "Branch of Hope" (with pastor Rich Agozino) started services the first week of December.

Twenty-five members of our two hundred person church left to begin the new work. We learned something about the ring that day. We let go of twenty-five brothers and sisters. God sent fifty to replace them on the very day they left.

Rich quit his job and we helped the new church support him. He supplemented this with some equity from his house.

The church met in Agozino's living room for several months, then moved to a park. A few weeks under a picnic shelter brought considerable growth, then they rented a nightclub that had gone defunct. When the City of Torrance put them out of the club, they returned to the park. This time, the City allowed use of the recreation building.

Growth brought pressure for facilities. Rich used to take me on outings, looking for possible locations We visited bank buildings, supermarkets, schools and whatever. They settled into a Seventh Day Adventist Church building for three years. Today the congregation numbers nearly 400. They meet in a school auditorium and are trying to buy a church building.

They have built and operated a boys' ranch and are responsible for a couple of other churches in Southern California.

God did a new thing through Rich Agozino. He taught us to plant churches and we've done it repeatedly ever since.

18

FILLED AND OVERFLOWING

Branch of Hope wasn't the only church with building problems. In 1971, when Ruby and I came to 1456 Manhattan Beach Boulevard to begin a church we found ourselves in a doll house. It was a perfect miniature church building, almost a toy. It had eight-foot by eight-foot classrooms designed for a teacher and two children. There were three of those little classrooms plus an office and a nursery. Each of them had the same tiny dimensions. Our auditorium held 72 people. The whole place was painted pink with the exception of the lavender nursery. We still had no people, but knew the building just wasn't going to work.

We improvised. I taught the Bible, verse by verse, in Sunday morning church. Everyone from junior high on up attended. Our Sunday School handled just the sixth graders and younger. We tore out walls, creating usable classroom space. Instantly, our tiny facility could accommodate a crowd three times larger than before. We also freed ourselves from an over-bearing, teacher-recruitment problem. All this due to a simple shift in philosophy.

A shift in philosophy can very often save you money.

As time went on, we filled the building, and since we couldn't stretch the building, we stretched our thinking. We packed 200 people into that little auditorium by knocking out the office and baptistery. On top of that, we invited everyone in Levi's to come sit on the rug surrounding me on the platform and in the aisles. If we had a special event we would open the windows and sit people outside on the patio or lawn behind the building. They enjoyed the service looking through the windows.

Talk about parking lots, ours was designed for seven cars. We did everything we could to make it work better. We tried valet parking for a while and were able to put twenty-five to thirty cars in there. We just jammed people everywhere. We parked on the lawn behind the building, we even tried to bus people back and forth from a nearby parking lot.

Our next move was to multiple services. That worked and we were able to expand further. We continued to try everything. We bought a house and used the garage for Sunday School, renting out the house to make payments. We bought a fourteen-foot by fourteen foot tin lawn shed from Montgomery Ward, and erected it beside the church to provide an instant Sunday School room.

Some generous people a block down the street gave us the use of a nursery school for about two years. After a time, though, the lady who managed the place would call us every Monday morning and throw us out. She would say we had left the place in a mess (we knew we hadn't), telling us we couldn't meet there anymore. One of our men would go down the hill, talk to her, calm her down and reinstate us. The owners were always on our side, the manager always against us. This went on for over a whole year.

Every week, we renegotiated ourselves back into that nursery school.

We did everything possible to exploit that tiny building. We got to where we could handle 350 people on Sunday morning but it wasn't enough. We were frustrated.

Meanwhile, there had been a struggle with the city. We had tried and tried to rent a Community Center two blocks away from us. The other Community Center in town was being used by another church, so we were certain the City wasn't opposed to churches. But every time we talked to the Recreation people, they would tell us that we couldn't use the Center due to budgetary problems. Our money would go to the City Treasury rather than the Recreation Department, but they would have to spend their own money to provide a custodian. Therefore, we couldn't use the building.

Finally, after about four years of annual applications to the Department, I talked to a girl who used to work for them. She told us their story was just a ruse to get us off their backs. She suggested that I write the mayor asking if someone was taking money under the table to allow the other church in the other Community Center. I was also to detail the past replies from the Recreation Department.

With much fear and trembling, I wrote the mayor and sent copies to the City Manager and Recreation Director. In three days the City Manager's Office called to tell us we could use the Community Center. The Recreation people were co-operative and everything worked out from there on. We never really knew why we had been held off for so long, as these people seemed glad when we finally moved in.

We rented that building for about a year and a half, holding one service on Sunday morning and one on Sunday evening. An earlier service met up the hill in the little church building. The congregation grew to about 450 people. We filled the Community Center to the place where we had to put people on tumbling mats stacked in the rear, after every chair they owned was used. Soon people were again outside looking through doors and windows. Frustration reigned eternal.

19

THE PROMISED LAND

Five days after we moved to Manhattan Beach, I was busy cleaning the church building when I was startled by someone crawling through the window. It turned out to be an old friend, Spencer Morris, whom I hadn't seen in several years. Spencer and I had hung around together in Oregon during our high school days. I had met him at church camp one summer. Although we attended the same church, we had never met. We were watching a baptism in the swimming pool, struck up a conversation and became friends. During the next couple of years, we dated the same girls, and had some good times together, but we were decidedly different.

Spencer was a daredevil. He never graduated from high school because he skipped school all the time. He missed more than half of his junior year to do such exciting things as fishing. He was the first person that I had ever ridden with who drove over a 100 miles an hour in an automobile. Spencer was an exciting person to be around.

I went away to college, and a year later he showed up. He had passed the high school equivalency test and they let him into college. He was the same old Spencer. He had fun and his school work suffered. He wasn't all that interested in what the teachers had to offer, but he was interested in serving the Lord.

Well, I'm cleaning the floor and Spencer comes crawling in the window. I nearly suffered a stroke. He was in between work and looking for some excitement. He heard about us starting a church and decided to come help.

Spencer moved into our house and I hired him to clean the church, lead songs and preach when I was out of town. After that time, both my wife and I had this vision in our hearts of a church numbering a couple of thousand people, even though we were operating in this little tiny building with only twenty people. Knowing this, Spencer showed up one afternoon declaring, "I found the building, I know the place that God wants us to meet in for church."

He drove me up the hill about a mile and a half to a huge piece of property that was horribly vandalized. We discovered it had been built as a bowling alley in 1960 at a cost of two million dollars. Eleven years later it was a huge vandalized waste. When the bowling alley went bankrupt, the bank had sold the pin setters and all other furnishings. It was just one large empty structure whose interior was one-third larger than the size of a football field. It had been built on pillars, with parking for 120 cars beneath.

We were certain we had found the "Promised Land" of our church. In fact, we were so certain that we publicly told people this was the place God wanted for us. Our feelings were reinforced by three separate elderly people who had noticed the structure going up a decade before and prayed that God would turn it into a church. They felt that perhaps it was being built for a church. When they discovered it wasn't, they prayed that God would turn it into one.

The vacant bowling alley had become a huge eyesore. After researching the property for a year, we finally wrote the owners and invited them to donate the structure for a tax write-off. As you might guess, they didn't even answer our letter.

Time went on, and the building became a sore spot for a couple of people in our church. They felt we should not grow, but remain small because churches belonged in homes or small homey buildings, not in big abandoned bowling alleys. But we continued to feel that God had led us to this place.

We were constantly faced with the need for space and looked into a number of other properties also. We would get all excited, trust the Lord for the bowling alley, pray for it and tell everybody in church we were on our way to the Promised Land. When the owners would reject our offer, we'd turn blue and look for other property. We repeated that cycle nineteen times.

We tried to buy four or five other churches and only got them mad at us in the process. We looked at industrial space, at vacant supermarkets and got into a race with the Federal government for a huge warehouse. We tried to buy a high school and junior high school. You name it. We knew the size of the property and how much it cost. We knew everything about every chunk of land in the South Bay.

It came down to either the bowling alley or Los Angeles Airport, nothing else was working. I guess you know no one was scrambling to sell us the airport.

I nearly got busted by the police praying for that building. One night after a men's fellowship, Dick Whittet, Jim Suarez and I drove to the bowling alley to ask the Lord for it. There we were at 11:30 P.M. laying hands on this brick wall praying that it would be ours and a police car drove up. The officer, it seemed, frowned on that sort of activity, at least after dark. We spent quite a bit of time with our knees knocking and voices trembling explaining what it was we were doing. They checked our ID's and our story about Hope Chapel. Their response was, "Hope Chapel, huh. That's a good church. You get this building. We want you to have this building. We're tired of chasing kids through here in the middle of the night." We read in the local newspaper that there had been several rapes and a policeman had been murdered in what we now call the Ocean View Room.

I remember attending a Pastors' conference in Colorado, praying my heart out that God would give us the building. We were pressured for space, and there was no place to go. We were making a difference in people's lives, and we knew God wanted to expand our ministry, but there was no room for more. There were eleven hundred people in this conference when the speaker asked us to turn to somebody that we had known for a while and pray with them. As I turned around, Jack Hayford waved at my wife and me and spoke a word of prophesy to us. I don't remember the statement exactly, but it went something like, "The Lord has established you as a tall coconut tree, standing on a hill overlooking the ocean. Don't think it strange that the Lord has compared you to a coconut tree. Its a very natural thing for a coconut tree to give off other small coconuts and those others grow into daughter trees, and the Lord will establish your comings and your goings." The significance of that prophecy was yet to be understood, but it seems the Lord was talking to us about establishing churches in the illustration of the coconut.

I really believe that Jack had spoken a word from the Lord to us, but I could only focus on the part about this coconut tree planted on a hill by the ocean. The bowling alley was on a hill overlooking the Pacific Ocean in Hermosa Beach.

Upon returning from the convention, I sat down and read the Los Angeles Times. In fact, I read through the last thirteen copies of the Los Angeles Times. Since I'd paid for them, I was going to read them. As I was doing this, my wife was browsing through the ads, clipping coupons. She came upon an advertisement describing several buildings at auction.

Among them was the bowling alley!

You have to understand how we felt. Just two days earlier Jack Hayford had given us this prophecy about being planted on a hill overlooking the ocean. Here I am, looking through my old newspapers and my wife suddenly discovers the bowling alley is up for auction. I was now certain that God was going to give us the building and that the timing of the prophecy and the newspaper discovery was no coincidence. God was working to give us the property.

We got all excited. I remember standing up in church, asking everyone to pray that we would obtain the building, and telling them that I was certain that God was taking us into the Land of Promise. We had been wandering around the wilderness for a long time. The doors were finally opening and we were going to move on into our Promised Land.

At that time, we were introduced to a man named Norman Hahn who had excellent credentials in real estate. He received an award from Governor Ronald Reagan in 1973 for selling more real estate than any other person in

California. In fact, he once sold an entire town including an airport. He was a wonderful Christian and had negotiated the Melodyland transaction in Anaheim. We felt we could really trust this man. It turned out we could. He gave us good advice, spent hours on our project as a ministry to us. There were four hundred of us in church on Sundays, but we had no money in the bank. Every dime we took in, we either spent on ministry or gave to someone in need. We were giving away 30% of our income. We were fearful of committing ourselves to the building with resources so tight. Paul Jones, who fills the role of Bishop over about 150 churches advised us to rearrange our priorities to insure the future existence of Hope Chapel. We were so bent on giving money away that we weren't insuring the future of the congregation. If we couldn't house the church, there would be no funds to give to the needy.

We calculated some cutbacks and projected the ability to make some payments. Norm felt that although the building had cost $1.8 million to build and had been for sale for over $400,000, we could buy it for a quarter of a million at auction. We had no way of touching that kind of money by ourselves, so we spoke to Paul Jones and the Foursquare people. They came through with flying colors. Dipping into their home missions fund, they gave us a certified check for 15 per cent of the $250,000 which was $37,500. This would tie up the property while they arranged a loan for us for the balance.

Despair loomed tall and ugly at the auction. With bated breath we sat around as the auctioneer set up his little table in front of the building. The ground swelled with onlookers, bidders and about a hundred Hope Chapel folks. At exactly ten o'clock the auctioneer brought down his gavel and opened the bidding.

The first and last bid was for $275,000. Twenty-five thousand more than our prearranged limit. A local entrepreneur and land developer planned to build racquetball courts in place of bowling lanes.

We were losers, locked out of our Promised Land. I cried in the alley behind the supermarket. I can remember exactly where I was sitting and what I was doing. I sat on the steps of the Lucky Market loading dock and watched this tall man in a blue suit walk beyond the cyclone fence through the broken glass doors and up the steps to survey his purchase.

I felt like a fool. I had to go back to the congregation and explain to them that I had led them down a primrose path to nowhere. I was a prophet that didn't know what he was talking about. We'd wound up with nothing but empty words.

I was so devastated that I would do anything I could to avoid the bowling alley. I didn't even want to see that place. If I was in someone else's car and they drove by, I would painfully look in the other direction. I can't describe to you the crippling feelings of emptiness and self-doubt. I would sit with my kids at McDonald's about a block away with my back to the bowling alley. I didn't even want to see the roof.

I felt like an absolute fool. I dove into the Scriptures, especially the story of David running from Saul. David had believed God was going to make him King in Jerusalem, now he pictured himself a hunted dog certain of his own impending destruction. I could identify with him.

It's been a couple of chapters since we talked about the ring. I need to confess that during those dark days I was simply feeling sorry for myself. I wanted control of my life and circumstances. I felt that God had told me something, that I had faithfully passed it on to others, but was left holding the empty bag. I raged against the possibility that I could be wrong. God had taken control of circumstance away from me and it was painful, nearly disastrous. I felt like quitting the pastorate. In fact, I wished I could die.

In the Bible, God forced everyone He blessed to relinquish that ring of power before He did His part. We cannot be gods unto ourselves and expect Him to work in our situation.

My problem was that while our people needed that bowling alley for a house of worship, I lusted for it to validate my perspectives. I wanted to say, "I told you so. I was right all along." God isn't really thrilled with that kind of attitude.

As I look back, the strangest part of the whole experience is that the building kept crowding its way back into my thoughts and conversation. I knew all those guys in the Bible suffered great loss of face before inheriting God's success. Abraham waited twenty five years for a promised son. At ninety-eight he laughed in God's face and explained biology to him a year before his son was born. He knew the impossible and tried to prove it. Joseph not only waited for God's promise, he spent the time in jail as an accused rapist. I guess I didn't have things so bad.

The stories of these men and others like them were hard to handle. I wanted to put the whole negative experience behind me, but those Old Testament patriarchs seemed to scream out, "Trust Him just a little longer!"

We weren't able to give up praying for this building! Roy Hicks recently said that we should learn to pray "until."   In other words, we should pray until God comes through. We should never give up on Him.

During the months after the auction I felt called to trust God for the building, even though it was on its way to becoming a racquetball club. I was exhausted and didn't want to pray. At least tomorrow would be predictable if we gave up hope. Continued trust requires peace in the midst of God's unpredictability.

20

BREAKTHROUGH

Santa Barbara is wonderful in the fall. The summer haze past, the whole town shimmers in the cool Autumn sun.

We went there to pray for direction. Each fall the pivotal leaders in our church would take time for a prayer retreat and return with plans for the future.

Someone spoiled the meeting when they spoke the obscene words, "bowling alley."

We'd already laughed and cried over the news that the city wouldn't allow racquetball courts due to a floor loading problem. We rejoiced that day, but the tears flowed when we tried to buy it from the new owner. He just wouldn't take us seriously.

We heard he was going to leave the building alone and untouched, a vandalized monument to the bureaucracy that overturned his sports complex.

Whatever his reasons, he wouldn't deal with us.

Norm Hahn would show up with an offer, the owner would promise to consider it and respond in a couple of days. His response was to raise the price or not call back at all. This went on for months.

When someone in our prayer meeting said "bowling alley," the rest looked like they were ready to pack up, head for L.A. and forget the retreat. It didn't turn out that way.

We talked awhile and prayed intensely one afternoon. That evening we worshipped Him in song. God gave us the plan we sought that night. God says that in all our ways we are to acknowledge Him and He will direct our paths. As we did that through song and praise, He came roaring through on our behalf.

God spoke to me and suggested that we enter into a different style of negotiation. We were to approach the owner and ask him if he would sell us the property, but allow him to name the price.

Let me tell you how it worked. I visited my parents on vacation that summer. While I was there, my dad bought a set of snow tires for his pickup truck. He found them advertised in the newspaper, and went out to visit the man who owned them. He looked over the tires, and found that they were in very good condition, almost brand new. He told the man, "Look, what's the lowest price you're willing to take? You name the price, and I'll go ahead and pay you that for the tires." The whole deal depended upon a trust that my father had built in this man in just a few moments time. Dad felt he could believe in him so he said, "I'll pay your price," even before he knew what it was. The man sold him the tires at a very favorable price. I must point out that the guy really had my father over the barrel. If he had been unscrupulous, we would have been in an embarrassing situation.

God told us to approach our promised land bowling alley in exactly the same manner as my father had bought the tires.

We wrote a letter to that effect and I signed it. The letter began: "Dear Sir, This is the most unusual letter you'll ever read...." We went ahead to promise this man that we would buy his property at whatever price he named. He would name the price and then say these words, "This is the lowest amount I'm willing to take for the property." There was no way that he could hold us to a contract with a really ridiculous price. But if the price was in the ballpark, we were committing ourselves in advance to the money.

We were so intent on vulnerability and trust that we sent along records of our cash flow for all the years we'd been in existence as a church. We wanted him to know exactly where we stood.

A couple of weeks later, I got a telephone call. The offer had been misunderstood. He thought that we were up to some trick and were trying to cheat him out of the building. When we began to understand each other, he got excited and decided to try and find a way to glean a tax advantage by donating it to our church.

In two days, he came back with an opportunity for us to buy the property at only $175,000, if we could move within thirty days. He would take a great tax loss on the property and it would benefit us.

We weren't ready, and just didn't have the ability to move that fast. So, he came up with another plan. Things had so turned around since that prayer meeting, the formerly reluctant owner was now a good friend.

He worked out a lease with an option to purchase, at a time when real estate prices were moving like a rocket. It was a sellers' market and lease options were simply not available.

We could lease for up to two years, with an option to purchase for only $350,000. He had lowered his price by $150,000. The payments were easy for us to work with. Within just a matter of months from that prayer meeting and God's direction to entrust ourselves to a stranger, God had worked things out for us in terms that were fair and easy. We began to remodel the building.

The remodeling project was done by faith. We signed the lease with only $4,000 in the bank and cash flow barely adequate to make the lease. In our naivete, we estimated that it would cost $30,000 to remodel the building; it wound up costing $250,000 just for the initial remodeling to occupy the structure.

The Lord worked gracious miracles during that period of time. We hired five men out of our church to work as full-time carpenters. If volunteers came, one or two carpenters would break off to supervise. We made pretty intelligent use of unskilled volunteer labor, something that I had never seen done before in a church. When we finished the project, our labor costs came in at 20 per cent of the remodeling price. They're usually about 50 per cent on any building.

We were ready to move in. God had supplied the money as needs arose. Every week we took in huge offerings, but they never contained huge checks. It was just that a lot of people gave more than they ever had before. The Lord took us through even though the project cost ten times what we estimated. God supplied the money right up to the point that we moved in. We moved in, cancelled the lease and bought the property all within six months after we drove the first nail.

The financial disaster hit about two weeks later. God has mysterious ways of keeping His people humble.

Our first Sunday at the new location attracted lots of attention. Our story made the South Bay Daily Breeze. The Los Angeles Times did a full page story and a television network covered "The Church in a Bowling Alley" with a three and one-half minute feature.

We got cocky, but the Lord was prepared for us. The offerings dropped right back to normal and although we had an Occupancy Certificate we hadn't completed the construction.

There was another complication. We had started to buy carpet at a discount from a legitimate carpet company through a friend in the church. Then we came across a better deal at a little hole-in-the-wall carpet shop in Venice. The man asked for $10,500 cash in advance, but when the carpet arrived from the mill it was marked C.O.D.

We couldn't understand what had happened, but we soon found out the guy had stolen our money. He gave us a sob story about how he'd been involved in the Holocaust and escaped a prisoner of war camp, and ever since his morals were corrupted and he just didn't know what to do. He had used the money to pay some other expense. He seemed like a helpless individual until we discovered that he had already transferred his business and home into his son's name so we couldn't touch them. Then as a precaution he went to church and went forward at an altar call. Someone had told him we wouldn't sue a Christian. We won a judgment against him; in fact, he voluntarily signed it against himself, but there was no way to touch his assets. He just took us to the cleaners.

But God used that to humble us. We found ourselves meeting for weeks in this church building with no carpet on the floor, no paint on the walls and no money to buy either. It was worse than it seems because the lack of carpet produced a horrible slapping echo when a sound was made.

We got off our high horse and learned to trust and pray again. Of course the Lord supplied our need.

21

THE SOAP SALESMAN

You meet all kinds of people in church. There are house-wives, bank operations people and lots of aerospace types in Hope Chapel. I've told you about bikers and small businessmen. Once a guy came confessing his dangerous and ill-fitted life of espionage.

The soap salesman, too, is a story that's worth telling.

Mind you, this isn't your average run-of-the-mill soap salesman. The guy was well-educated and had been around.

He had graduated from USC, then traveled through Europe and Asia on the Hashish Trail. After that he opened a pharmacy in Kona, Hawaii. While handling legitimate drugs in the pharmacy, he bought and operated a marijuana farm in the mountains for two years. Then he discovered soap.

Our hero quit his two drug businesses for a pyramid-structured soap company, the kind that sells more dealer-ships than soap. It was more lucrative. He had three pyramids going with lots of people working for him when he visited Hope Chapel in the Community Center.

For his wife it was a stab at saving their marriage, but for him, all a church could offer was more business contacts.

He only lasted two weeks. Not that he ran out of contacts, he ran into me. I was telling the church we were going to move to the bowling alley. Though we'd lost it at auction, God has given us "this wonderful plan to contact the new owner...." The guy thought I was nuts and he didn't want to get tainted. He'd sell soap elsewhere.

Almost a year went by before we saw each other again.

One afternoon he came home to an empty house. His wife even took the. phone. The front door stood open, waving mockingly in the breeze. He would have done violent harm if he had been able to find her, but that wouldn't be easy as he had hitchhiked home. She had stolen his Seville off the street.

His wife made off with his business partner and this was one angry soap salesman.

By nightfall, the anger turned to hurt and in that empty house he turned his life over to Jesus Christ. He had already noticed, with some consternation, that Hope Chapel now occupied the old bowling alley on top of the hill. The next morning Zac Nazarian showed up for church.

Of course, we had no idea he would one day pastor the church, but we all took to him.

Two things stood out in the man. First was devotion. He attended every service. I would even try to change my message between the eight and ten o'clock services just so he wouldn't get bored. Zac soaked up the Word like a dry sponge in water. The second characteristic was integrity. He forgave his wife and gave her his home and all his business interests. He "turned the other cheek," because the Lord said he should.

22

MISTAKES AND MERCEDES

"They entered the promised land and lived happily ever after."

That statement wasn't true in ancient Israel and it surely didn't describe us. We really thrashed around after the move. First, we had the financial crisis. Our offerings had returned to pre-project level. The guy stole the carpet money and we kept on spending. One day we found ourselves up to our Bibles in red ink.

Our leadership team was made up of a bunch of guys who were long on faith and love, but lacked experience in resource management. We hadn't tracked our spending and now we were in trouble. Big trouble! Within ten days, we needed twenty thousand dollars more than we had, just to pay local hardware and building suppliers.

The Lord came through from three directions. A ship captain had accepted the Lord months earlier. When he heard of the news, he gave us an ocean view lot he had bought for his dream home. The equity met half the need.

The Foursquare Denomination gave us a cash gift and a loan, completing the bailout. The third blessing was a man named Don Stewart.

Don spent his life in aerospace engineering and management. He came on our pastoral team, ironed out our plans and taught us to manage. He has been an anchor to us, and God has used Don's steady hand to insure the success of many grand schemes of ministry.

Financial needs are one thing, pride problems are quite another.

In our early days people scoffed at "that bunch of hippies" and wouldn't associate with us. Now we were in the limelight and socially acceptable. It went to my head.

The media attention was hard enough to handle, but one day I noticed Mercedes and Cadillacs where the crusty Volkswagens had been. Someone even drove a Rolls Royce to church.

We hadn't changed congregations. The church had simply grown to where we could minister to the middle class as effectively as students and street people.

I remember discussing image and impression with one of our staff guys. We decided to take a little more "uptown" approach to ministry. We needed class.

Remember Jesus? He said that He would build His church and that pastors should feed the sheep. Well, I took over His role and schemed to build the church. We "grew" from 800 people to 600 and holding.

We had exploded with growth for a few weeks after the move. Then I took over and we started losing. I usurped the Lord's place, grabbed onto that "ring of control" and wouldn't let go.

No one even stopped to consider that all the new people had come because the Lord sent them, and that they would keep coming if we held steadfastly to our ministry pattern.

Instead, we generated elaborate new programs to hold people and bind them in.

The Kentucky Fried Chicken people proudly declare, "We do chicken right." They imply that they are the best at chicken because they don't dilute their efforts with every other fast food. We used to "do equipping right," but we abandoned that role for everything we could conceive that would cause growth. We ended up doing nothing right.

There is a clear pattern in the New Testament for church growth. The elders reinforce themselves by "devoting themselves to prayer and the Word. (Acts 6:4)" Then those leaders become a gift to the church for "equipping the saints for the work of the ministry. (Ephesians 4:12)" This equipping goes on as the church meets regularly for teaching, fellowship, breaking of bread (communion) and prayer. Strengthened in the Spirit, the individual Christians penetrate, flavor, preserve and influence their culture. In the process of their declaration of the Gospel, "The Lord adds to the church such as should be saved. (Acts 2:47)"

We ignored that plan for several years. We could describe it in glowing terms, but we weren't practicing it.

Because of our history, people were researching our "rapid growth" for doctoral dissertations. I regularly spoke at Robert Schuller's Church Growth Institutes. The problem? It was history. We weren't growing in numbers and I believe it's only hypocritical to say we grew spiritually. Healthy sheep breed more sheep. As I look back, I feel we detoured upon moving to our current location, if not before. We got our eyes off of people and onto facilities, then onto program.

After languishing for two years, we finally got back on track.

23

ON THE REBOUND

I gave up trying to pastor a "big church" and went back to being myself. I prayed for direction and the Lord told me to tend His flock.

Communication had broken down and I didn't even know the flock. People could be in the church for two years and only be recognized as newcomers. There was no network of relationship. It wasn't so bad if I didn't recognize people, but it was terrible that no one did. We knew we needed a small-church mentality, and that we should subdivide the congregation to get it.

But how? Three past attempts were proven failures.

One day, Craig Englert, one of our pastors, came in all excited about something going on in a little church we helped start in Honolulu. The three pastors had divided the congregation into three groups, and on Sunday night they met in separate homes for Bible studies. They had replaced a regularly scheduled church service with small groups. It worked as people were beginning to know each other a little better and ministry took place almost spontaneously. They learned to serve each other.

We gathered the leaders of our church for a church growth conference at one of our daughter churches, New Life Fellowship in Culver City. John Amstutz, on staff at L.I.F.E. Bible College and Fuller Seminary, helped us assess the strengths and weaknesses of our church. We compared this to seven characteristics of growing churches. After grading Hope Chapel individually, we gathered to discuss our ratings. It was nearly unanimous that we needed a small-group encounter in the middle of the week where people could share their problems and victories, and get to know one another. The small groups should replace a regular service, like they had done in Hawaii, so people would know we were serious.

We prayed for a week, then had a meeting of what I called the "undershepherds." This included everybody I could identify operating as any kind of leader in our church. This included 150 of our 600 people. I gathered everyone that I could see influencing the life of somebody else, even if this person was rebellious toward the authority of the church. If he was influencing somebody else, I assumed that he was a leader and that God had given him some ability to lead people. He was in fact, shepherding the flock along with me. Talk about surrender; I had to admit I wasn't the whole show.

At the meeting we presented a proposed solution to our problem. Our whole church staff, plus Pat Hamman, the director of a camping program for handicapped kids, and John Woolheather, a former pastor, would pastor what we called MiniChurches. They would be just that, miniature churches, focused on people's needs and potential. If nothing else, someone would know your name if you came to our church and joined a MiniChurch.

We were back where we started. I pastored pastors and recognized that they pastored the church. It worked before and it works now.

We work hard at building the saints through teaching on Sunday and in MiniChurch. We share Communion on Sunday, but it is best at MiniChurch. People not only fellowship, they give testimonies and exercise spiritual gifts at MiniChurch.

As I write this book, there are twenty-eight MiniChurches. There would be more but several have broken off to form Hope Chapels, in Venice, Hawthorne, Westchester and soon in Kailua, Oahu. MiniChurch is also an effective learning-by-doing pastor training ground.

The week before MiniChurch began, eighty-five people showed up to listen to my Wednesday night Bible study. The next week, 380 went to seven MiniChurches. Today we don't really know how many people attend MiniChurch, but over seven hundred came to a prayer meeting announced only to MiniChurch pastors.

24

VISIONS OF TOMORROW

Hope Chapel is really moving. Watching its rising momentum has been a bittersweet experience for me. Solomon said honey on the tongue will make a weary man's eyes shine. My eyes shine over God's work in the church I pastor. The people are lovely, faithful and a joy to my heart.

There is a sadness though and it crept in just as the church got back in the groove.

In May 1978, Dick Whittet and I were walking down near the beach in Hermosa. He told me the Lord had asked him to pray for me every day. Dick and his family were preparing to plant a Hope Chapel in Bozeman, Montana at the time and he told the Lord, "Ralph should be praying for me, instead."

He said the Lord assured him I needed the prayer support and he wanted me to know he was praying.

Six weeks later I took my family on vacation to Hawaii. On the way over, as I walked up the aisle of the airplane (if you must know, I was headed for the rest room, not a very "spiritual" moment), I saw a vision. Now I don't take visions lightly. I have experienced very few and probably would doubt you if you said you'd had one. Nevertheless, I saw a vision.

I was alert to my position in the plane, but I could envision myself in the clouds looking down upon myself standing among a number of Asian people in a place that looked like Kaneohe, Oahu. It was strange, as though I were in all three places at once.

Also strange was our size. The people, myself included, were of normal size. The territory, however, seemed shrunken to about one third the size of a football field.

Two terms came to mind: "dominant" and "five years." I questioned the word dominant as descriptive of any ministry. We are supposed to be servants. The "five years," though, seemed an indication that I was to live out the picture five years later.

The entire vision could not have taken more than three seconds. I immediately dismissed it as momentary hysteria.

I knew God had called me to spend my whole life with a group of people in California identified as Hope Chapel. Furthermore, visions can be misleading. Especially to a person that loves Windward Hawaii for its green, wet, humid beauty and has just come from an exciting week with twelve hundred Japanese American Christians. The previous week I had taught College and Career Focus at the Annual Summer Camp for JEMS (Japanese Evangelical Missionary Society).

I knew the so-called vision had to be a trick of my psyche or worse. Maybe the devil was trying to distract me from the work the Spirit was doing at Hope.

I forgot the whole thing. I forgot it so well that I hardly remembered it when Dick Whittet brought it up at the end of my vacation.

We were gone for three weeks, and flew the "red eye" home so we could squeeze an extra five hours into our trip. The plane landed at six a.m. on Friday and I had to preach that night at seven. I couldn't sleep, so I went to the church at noon to open my mail.

Around four p.m., tired and crabby, I encountered Dick who asked, "Did anything unusual happen on your trip? Remember, I've been praying for you. The Lord told me that on your vacation you would be lifted up in the air and given a vision of your future." I laughed him off. I looked at my watch and said, "It's four o'clock. My vacation is officially over at seven, so if God has any visions for me, He'd better hurry!"

About ten after six, it hit me. I almost dropped the peas off my fork. Dick had described the vision I saw three weeks earlier. I had been lifted up, both literally and figuratively in that vision and shown a picture of my future. I found Dick and apologized for my smart attitude. I also swore him to secrecy.

My Master's program at California Graduate School of Theology required a thesis. I wrote a dissertation length paper on the History of Christianity among Japanese-Americans in Hawaii. I wanted to learn everything I could.

I still told no one except my friend Aaron Suzuki.

Aaron was born in Maui. He grew up both in Hawaii and on the Mainland. He was a real doper and carouser before he got saved. An engineer at American Honda, Aaron was planning suicide. The afternoon of the big day, he asked Jim Doehla, a Charismatic Lutheran and co-worker, why he was so happy. Jim took him out and read Romans to him from the New Testament. Aaron says it was all Greek to him, but his heart opened and he asked Jesus into his life.

Jim thought Aaron too much a swinger for the Lutheran Church, so he brought him to a Hope Chapel baptism on New Year's Eve, 1973.

Aaron had felt God might be calling him to pastor, particularly among Japanese-Americans. Maybe in Hawaii. I shared the vision and he didn't think I was crazy. He even read through my very long Master's Thesis. We prayed long and were assured God was calling us to Hawaii to plant churches.

New challenges are always exciting, and I thrive on adventure, but this endeavor involved the pain of leaving dear friends and familiar circumstances. Bittersweet indeed.

Ken Hiroshige hit me with his wisecrack about letting go of the ring a little prematurely.

I knew I would be leaving Hope and told Ken long before I announced it in church. It was also long before I could feel the pain, so his comment seemed unreal. It actually signaled a great struggle.

The church grew two and a half times in the years immediately following the establishment of MiniChurch.

We pioneered churches from Hawaii to Montana to Texas during that time. Several of them started churches in neighboring localities. I said goodbye to many friends. Dave Benefiel went to Moorpark, California. Dick Whittet to Montana. We lost Will Heinle to Fallbrook, California, Barry Felis went to Huntington Beach, Dan Boyd pastors Hope Chapel Del Rey, Craig Englert started three churches in Maui, and Pat Hamman is in Redmond, Washington. The list goes on and on.

Each time someone left with a team to start a church I'd feel a little sad, but I never connected those feelings with my own departure.

One day it hit. Hard.

I was heading home with my family one autumn day, driving an old Porsche I'd restored. We had just come from surfing and sitting around in the sun at Bank Wright's house on the beach. We'd had great fellowship talking about the Lord.

Afternoon shadows were lengthening and the Santa Ana winds blew warm. I plunged into depression: "I don't want to leave all this, I can't." My good friends from the church, the warm weather with its fall smells of smog and Coppertone, even the Beach Boys playing on cassette seemed to cry out against my leaving. The whole scene represented everything I held dear and it all seemed threatened by the move. I spent roughly the next four months fighting depression.

To make things worse we took another wave of media attention a couple of months later. They were interested in a church that was reaching surfers and beach people. We hit the major networks and a UPI story showed up as far away as Toronto and Florida. I never handle good publicity all that well anyway, but this time it was reinforcing just how good life was in California.

I really struggled during those months. I didn't want to leave security, notoriety, good friends and all that makes home lovely for the relative insecurity, obscurity and uncertainty of life in another state.

If control of your circumstances could be symbolized by the ring in Tolkien's books, I wanted to wear mine. Forget letting go. I prayed and I cried until one day the Lord took away the feelings.

Aaron and I were surfing in front of Bank's house on a warm winter morning when someone mentioned how the conditions reminded them of Hawaii. I poured out my feelings about leaving the certainty of life in California for an undescribed future far away.

My friends reminded me that I hadn't known the future in 1971, but had moved to South Bay with little more than my family and faith in the Lord. If He had been trustworthy then, wasn't He now?

I gave in. I let go of the ring and the Holy Spirit gave me a whole new set of feelings. He also cracked the door just enough for us to see what might lay down the road.

I found out that an old friend, Dr. Robert Chang was the honorary Mayor of Kaneohe. I was looking for contacts for musical help for our first week in Hawaii when my entertainer friend Carole Kai phoned to let me know she had moved to the Mainland. She and her husband, Dennis, had been in our church for a couple of weeks. Beside the musical help both provided, Dennis and I have become great friends. We wanted to buy time on Christian radio in Hawaii. KAIM, the main Christian station, gave us an evening traffic slot, sandwiched between Mike MacIntosh and Chuck Smith, two of the most popular teachers in their format.

When you finally give in and give God authority, He will use and bless you beyond your wildest dreams. He did it for Abraham, David, Paul and the rest of them. As you read this, He's doing it for me.

God doesn't want you to give up. He isn't playing Pac Man with your life. He's not interested in robot Christians.

Do you remember the Centurion talking to Jesus in Matthew 8:9? He said, "I am a man under authority." God wants you and me to be people under His authority. Not robots, just good soldiers of the cross.

Letting go of the ring suggests we let go of our designs of power, crawl off the throne and let Him have His rightful place of authority. God doesn't want you to give up, He wants you to give in.

25

LET GO AND LET ZAC

I guess the book ended with the last chapter, but if you have a few minutes I'd like to tell you about a real neat favor from the Lord.

His name is Zac Nazarian. For five years I prayed that God would bring a smooth transition in leadership when I moved on. I ran track in college and remember all too well losing a relay race because someone dropped the baton during the hand off. The act symbolized the way many churches change pastors. They fumble and stumble, losing precious time if not the race.

When Zac came back from seminary, we hired him part-time as a counselor. He was to fill in the rest of his time as a pharmacist.

Not Zac. His new wife, Julie, flew for an airline so they could get by with their combined salaries. We caught up to him as his schedule hit 55 hours a week.

He gave himself to the ministry like no one I knew except possibly Don Stewart. Counseling is hard on the emotions, so I teased him about being a masochist. I also restricted him to a forty-five hour schedule and gave him a raise.

He had come back as an intern and we had thoughts of sending him to Palos Verdes to pastor in two years.

Zac is a real learner and I noticed he was buying into everything we stood for. We have a philosophy of ministry that God has forged in us over the years. Too often our people go away to study and upon return they can't reconcile their book knowledge with our practical position. Zac was Hope Chapel from start to finish. I attributed that to the fact he had started and pastored a house church while attending seminary. His knowledge was tempered with experience.

One day I told him I was leaving and thought God wanted him to take my job.

He was incredulous, told me I was crazy and almost walked out. I persisted. Up to this time I had only discussed the idea with Tom McCarthy and Tom had agreed heartily.

Tom is an obstetrician and a great preacher. He filled the pulpit whenever I was away, the people loved him and our elders had an unwritten understanding that if I died or became disabled Tom would take my place.

Tom and I felt certain Zac was the guy. Zac was sure that we were nuts. When I told the church council my intentions to leave, the first words in reply were, "Who's going to take your place, Zac?"

God blessed the church with Zac. More than that, he blessed me with Zac. This was a man after my own heart.

For a year he has administered our life at Hope Chapel even sending out three new churches, and has done all the Sunday evening teaching. As I write, he has been the "new pastor" in the pulpit for four Sunday mornings. Sunday evening attendance has been up for a year and now Sunday morning crowds are growing.

That bothers me a little. The old ego is a little bruised. On the other hand, I rejoice with all my heart.

I'm not really leaving, but being sent from Hope Chapel Hermosa Beach as an apostle to plant churches. For our success in Hawaii we need a strong home base and we have it.

All that benefits me greatly, but it cost me something as well. We hoped we could hand off the baton in a way other churches could model. No cold surprises. Our church knew eighteen months in advance of the transition. They got to sample Zac, to get used to him, but only as I was willing to step down and give him room to operate. Stepping down was painful but it paid off. It always does.

You might be interested to know that I went to the dentist last week. My mouth was propped open wide with all kinds of hardware inside while I was fitted for a crown. No chance for me to answer. Dr. Ken said, "Hey I'm proud,of you Frodo, you really did it, you let go of the ring...."

26

WAS IT WORTH IT?

Four years have come and gone and people still ask me the same question. People ask it until it wearies me.

Was it worth it? The answer is always the same and will never change.

Of course it was worth it!

Obedience to God is always worth it. You cannot lose your life, by seeking to do so for His sake. You only lose by trying to cling to it.

Usually the questioner is wondering if Hawaii is really a nice place to live and is not so concerned with the element of obedience. Hawaii is a lovely place to live, but so was California. The only real issue is whether you are walking in obedience to the Spirit. No matter how good or bad the physical surroundings, the only paradise this world offers is a walk in the Spirit. Four years ago, my family and a few good friends moved nearly three thousand miles. We set up housekeeping in a place that was new and foreign to us. We all felt a little like Abraham as we packed our bags and headed for a land the Lord would show us. It was a costly and painful change but very worthwhile.

Let me tell you about it...

Besides all the great stories of new friends and warm experiences, there are tangible spiritual results. The Kingdom of God has grown. Because we moved to Hawaii, new churches exist in eight locations in this state and two elsewhere.

We began Hope Chapel Windward in September, 1983.

Aikahi Christian Fellowship got off the ground with our help five months later. Pastor Mike Hubbard lived in the islands working with another ministry. God put it in his heart to pioneer a church, but he lacked the commitment and backing of his friends. Through our friendship, the Lord brought the church to birth. Several people who were attending our fellowship joined with Mike and Joy.

One of those was a couple, Paul and Susan Hilker who came to Hawaii with us from Hermosa Beach. The Hilkers assisted Mike during the early days in Aikahi and then moved on to Texas. They now pastor Hope Chapel Foursquare Church in Carrollton, a suburb of Dallas. Helping us, and then Mike, provided the education and the impetus for starting that church.

A year after we started, our first minichurch pastor and worship leader, Sonny Shimaoka, and his wife, Sharon, assumed the pastorate of a church in Kona on the Big Island. The church had lost their pastors and shrunk to a membership of only seven people. That congregation now numbers nearly three hundred people and exerts a very strong influence on the spiritual life of the Big Island.

A year after Sonny started, a mutual friend of ours and a neighbor to Shimaokas, Greg Kirschmann and his wife Sandy started Keauhou (now Holualoa) Chapel in Kona. Greg, the former associate pastor of Faith Fellowship on

Oahu, brings years of valuable experience and confidence to the ministry.

While Sonny ministers to a large family of local folks, Greg reaches transplanted mainlanders. The two pastors are great friends and Kona will never be the same because of them.

That's not the end of our Big Island story. Just two months ago, Tony and Chris Rivera left Hope Chapel Kona to start Hope Chapel Foursquare Church in the little town of North Kohala. From the start, God granted them tremendous success and impact. They have already become one of the larger churches in their whole district.

Tony is a building contractor who hunts wild boar for a hobby. He goes after these dangerous animals with nothing more than a dog and knife. It takes no genius to guess that he has the respect of the men in the community. The exciting truth is that people respect Tony more for being a dependable man of God than for his carpentry skills or hunting courage.

Back on Oahu, two other exciting new churches grew out of Hope Chapel Windward while those guys were building on the Big Island.

Chuck Sironen, with his wife Kathy, began a little more than a year ago in a school cafeteria in Pearl City. The church quickly became one of the more solid congregations in our network. Chuck is still working very successfully in another career. We all look forward to the day when the rapidly growing church will claim him as their full-time pastor.

In Waikiki, Jack and Marie Nordgren pastor Hope Chapel in a local community center. They reach out to the residents who live in the shadow of tourist hotels, with the constant hustle and bustle of the resort world around them. Jack, a former street evangelist and follow-up man for the Waikiki Beach Chaplaincy, is particularly suited to that mission field.

There is even an outpost in Okinawa because we came to Hawaii. John Baccigalupo received Christ in Okinawa over a dozen years ago in a spectacular, though disconcerting, manner. A dyslexic, he had no access to God through His word and had not found Him in a very traditional church.

His marriage had gone sour. Life in the Marine Corps was not fulfilling. He found no solace in drugs. Minutes away from suicide at the barrel of his service revolver, John heard God tell him to read the Bible. John argued that he could not. He was still dyslexic. God persevered.

In anger, John picked up the Bible to prove his point. To his amazement he could read! Most appropriately, he fell on his knees and surrendered his life to Jesus.

John still cannot write without help from his wife, but he graduated from college last summer.

He and his wife, Tosh, ran our Christian Education program for more than a year before moving to pioneer a ministry back in Okinawa. They began the fellowship with Bible studies for Japanese hungry to practice English. This group has grown into a healthy and exciting family of Christians. This growing congregation now holds Sunday services in their own furnished building.

The hundreds of people who populate these congregations walk in fellowship with each other and the Lord because a few people trusted God and let go of their own personal security.

It really does pay to let go of the ring.

These new churches place a high value on personal evangelism, so they further the cause of Christ more rapidly and obey the Great Commission at a faster pace. Thus, the faster we pioneer churches, the better chance we have of introducing large numbers of people to Jesus. Even if those churches are small in their beginnings.

Consider if we had never left California. Hope Chapel in Hermosa Beach would probably be the same size it is now. We would probably have commissioned the same number of pastors in the last three years. We would probably be considered successful. But Hawaii, Japan and Texas would remain untouched by us. The Body of Christ would be smaller.

The results that come from obedience are exciting when you take time to consider them!

Not only did we trust God in coming here, but so did a whole congregation of people on the mainland. They funded us, they prayed faithfully, they even gave up their pastors and friends.

Everyone paid a price for the gospel.

However, there were several costs to the venture that we did not anticipate. Communication between daughter churches on the mainland broke down for awhile. It took a year for us to realize that Zac was in no position to travel around while he learned his new pastorate. I was too far away to do much good. The problem is resolved. Zac came up with a program to tie everyone together back at the home base, but we hurt in the interim.

A few people could not understand why a pastor would leave a large happy church. They believed that we were all mad at each other. That really hurt.

The homesickness was more painful than I ever imagined. This was especially true missing people we knew well, but not well enough for them to come visit.

Our children had to adjust to new schools and new friends. But God has been very good to them throughout the process. Both Carl and Kelly have made wonderful new friends and are doing great in school. A side bonus is that they enjoyed the excitement of a new church and both are very involved in ministry.

Hawaii isn't paradise any more than California or any other beautiful location. At times I've questioned whether I really heard from God at the beginning of this venture. Life goes on and it contains struggles that make it interesting, as well as painful. I wouldn't try to avoid them for a minute. I followed God and inherited a mixed bag of victory and uncertainty. There are no paradises, no primrose lanes in this world, only the joy of obedience.

The move was, and is, well worth it!

27

PROGRESS IN HERMOSA BEACH

It's funny how the Lord has to move His people around to accomplish His purposes.

The past four years have proven an old theory of mine. I don't believe any leader is capable of everything and I do believe God raises up different people for different times.

Roughly translated, that means that God had me in Hermosa Beach for the first stage in the life of that congregation. He anointed Zac Nazarian to take them through the second major growth period of their life as an assembly.

He works today much like He did in ancient Israel. Moses brought the nation out of bondage in Egypt, but it was Joshua that led them to occupy Palestine. Not too much later, it was David who brought them respectability and set the tone for the reign of Jesus as Messiah.

The congregation at Hermosa Beach is where they are today only because God sent me to another place and brought them His man for this hour. I say that with no lack of self-confidence. I simply believe that God called me as a pioneer and that He equipped Zac as an organizer and developer. Neither of us would be much good in the other's role.

Zac almost immediately led the congregation into a building program. The idea was so visionary that I thought it a mistake when I first heard about it. But after a couple of hours and several cups of coffee, I was convinced he was hearing God. The need to enlarge the facility is obvious by the overcrowding at every service. What other church has its Sunday morning services duplicated five times to capacity crowds? What other church defines "Sunday morning" as Friday evening plus Saturday evening, and then holds one of its three actual Sunday morning services off-campus to overcome the logistics of moving vast crowds in and out of its parking lot. The expanded facilities are a must!

The plans call for a five-phase expansion program. They will pay construction costs in cash. The project will move forward as the money comes in.

Hope Chapel Hermosa will soon be able to accommodate a congregation of five thousand people.

The first phase of the program will include relocation of the Children's Church to a spacious two-story facility behind the current auditorium. This will release the current children's area to become a 450 person multipurpose area for weddings, meetings, brunches and overflow from the "Sunday" services.

The second construction phase will push the front of the building onto the sidewalk along Pacific Coast Highway. They badly need room for new offices and counseling areas. Few people have any grasp of how many people it takes to serve others in a large church. One study suggests that a growing church requires one pastoral staff person as well as one support staffer per 150 people.

Phase three will make life a little easier for everyone. It includes a three-level underground parking structure. This will mean no more long walks in the rain to get to church on winter evenings. It will also mean that one acre of ground will support one acre of church building as well as three acres of parking. That's stewardship!

The fourth phase will be the "goodie." The auditorium will get enlarged to 1358 seats (910 of them on the first floor and the rest in a balcony). The Ocean View Room will expand to fit 250. They will gain an additional 29 new classrooms and the building will finally get an air conditioning system.

All that expansion will call for more parking. The final addition will be a new five-level parking garage holding 450 cars. It's going on the four house lots the church is purchasing just south of the building.

As I write, they still await construction. Lots of cash has come in and the church is ready to build. All that is needed is for the city to make up its mind who is going to pay for moving a large water line around the block. The water is for extra fire safety sprinkler systems. Once the permit comes through, the project will proceed.

However, it wouldn't even begin if I was still the pastor. I have a natural aversion to building programs and all the disruption they create. I have no trouble believing God to create a congregation out of nothing. Nor do I have trouble believing God to meet its needs with almost invisible resources. But the very idea of raising all that cash frightens me. Another reason why God has me here and Zac there.

I called California to clarify some information and I found out that the church has just today put in an offer to buy the supermarket next door. The offer was invited by the company that owns the market, so no one is just dreaming. Obtaining the market would allow the church to meet its building needs in one simple project; Children's Church, new auditorium, parking lot and all. Ever since we bought the bowling alley in 1976 we felt that God would one day give us that supermarket.

The old saying, "you can't steer a ship that is not moving," seems appropriate here. The move to enlarge the existing facilities got the ship moving. Maybe the Lord wants to steer it into calmer waters. I am excited to see what the future holds.

What excites me most is that the leadership of Hope Chapel in Hermosa has continued with the vision to plant churches.

They have some huge successes in this area, too. Since I left Hermosa, successful new congregations have sprung up in many cities around the West.

Randy Sanford, who preached the Sunday evening services for the past three years left for Denver to plant a church. He is already daily on the radio, and has a large group of people meeting informally. The prognosis is for a fast-growing new church in that community.

Bob Mallord used to deal cocaine. Now he pastors Hope Chapel in Venice, California.

Gary Sinardi pioneered our first church in Salt Lake City, Utah.

Dale Yancy and Jeff Fischer started a church with a group of people Jeff led to the Lord in Northridge, California. Jeff is now their pastor. Dale is pioneering in New Hampshire.

Steve Mullen began a counseling center and built a church from that base in Sandy, Utah.

The three newest ventures are much closer to home. Mark Keever, a transplanted Hawaiian, started in Gardena with over 300 people the first Sunday.

There is another strong new ministry nearby. Don Shoji began Hope Chapel in the Holiday Inn in Torrance. They now have almost 400 people and a long-term lease on an industrial building.

Bill Gross, a former worship leader, began Hope Chapel Redondo Beach just two months ago, but already they are nearing one hundred in fellowship.

Follow-up support to the daughter churches became an immediate difficulty when I left for Hawaii.

Zac could oversee those pastors who left under his ministry. But he could hardly be expected to input to the lives of men who began pastoring before he got saved. Most of them looked to him for leadership, but he felt inadequate. Zac is a humble man. He once told me that I was like a spiritual father to them while he was merely a stepfather.

The problem is now well in hand with the development of something called Hope Chapel Masters Program. Once a month, Zac brings in a highly qualified instructor to sharpen the skills of our pastors. Tapes of the sessions are mailed to those outside of driving distance. The program has proven an invaluable supplementary education addressing such issues as church finance, the pastor's home life, stress avoidance, discipline and ethics.

The mother church is not suffering from the birthing process. Each week large numbers of people express newfound faith in the Lord through the prayer time at the end of the services. The people of Hope Chapel do a fantastic job witnessing of Jesus' love to their friends and relatives.

That witnessing pays off in rapid-fire commitments to the kingdom of God. Every six weeks, over one hundred people publicly acclaim their faith through baptism in the "big hot tub" in the auditorium.

New ministries are sprouting up everywhere you look. When I attended services there, I was overwhelmed by the hundreds of square feet of bulletin boards it takes to keep all the ministry groups in touch with each other.

There is a ministry to Khmer refugees that has helped develop churches among Cambodians living in Long Beach.

The ski club meets just for fun; both when the snow flies in the winter and behind big fast water ski boats in the summer.

I recently picked up a piece of literature about a ministry group called "Breakaways." I discovered this was not the name for the prison ministry. It is a bicycle club that gets together for weekend fellowship rides as well as serious competition.

As a ministry to prisoners in the California State Penitentiary at Chino and in the Terminal Island Federal Penitentiary, the church has begun an effort known as "70 x 7." The name comes from Jesus' words in Matthew where He tells Peter that we should forgive someone "seventy times seven" and then some.

You can best understand the effect of the ministry through the words of inmate letters written as thanks for a weekend seminar at Chino earlier this year.

An inmate named Jonathan received Jesus during the seminar. He writes,

".... that I happened to be here at Chino, I feel is beyond coincidence and I thank the Lord and 70 x 7 for this blessing. I've been born again for one week now and already I can see a change...."

Another inmate named Kenneth says,

".... I think that the seminar finally gave the inmates here an alternative to organizations like the Mexican Mafia, etc. for survival in a maximum security prison and, ultimately, a way to stay out of prison once released...."

You might remember to pray for the man who did not sign his letter. He writes,

"I know there's a jungle out there waiting for me to fall in the quicksand which I dread very much. I only wish I had found Jesus just like all of you have and I feel I am missing so very much because of all these past years Satan has turned me into a sick, hateful alcoholic. I want to change my life for God's sake and mine and I know I will!"

70 x 7 is indeed an exciting ministry opportunity and one directly commanded by the Lord in the gospels. The results go both ways. Besides the 41 inmates that opened their hearts to the Lord on that seminar weekend, several of the volunteers from the church wrote things like,

"for the first time in my life, I really felt I was denying self and representing the love of Jesus. I knew I was where Jesus wanted me to be, presenting HIS LOVE to another human being. It was like a shock running through me."

Events like these are life changers for everyone involved.

The church is maturing in other areas as well. There is now a well-defined and effective team of volunteers organized for hospital visitation. This ministry is very important to the six or seven church members in local hospitals during any given week.

"Free To Choose" is a twelve-step fellowship for anyone who wants freedom from compulsive behavior. They minister to people suffering from drug addiction, alcoholism, overeating, bulimia, etc. The ministry builds on the assumption that helping others is the best way to help yourself.

In their words,

".... let's face it, most of us who suffer with compulsive behavior are very self-obsessed. Service helps release us from the nagging self-obsession which destroys our serenity. It is a way for us to give back to others some of what we have received. 'Give and it shall be given unto you.'"

The list goes on and on: ministry in Mexico, new-found hope for homeless people, services held on skid-row. A plan exists to start a Spanish-speaking church in South Bay. I even heard of a plan to start another church for hard-core beach people right in Hermosa Beach.

Hope Chapel has proven itself. Too often we hear of churches in trouble after a long-tenured senior pastor leaves. This congregation has only grown in grace and in vision.

He won't own up to it, but a lot of that has to do with a man named Zac Nazarian. Only now, after three years, will he admit he even feels like the pastor. It is quite obvious to the rest of us that God chose the right man and that the man walks in serious obedience to his Master. We all win for it!

28

CHURCH ON THE BEACH

Church on the beach! Sounds like fun, huh?

Let me tell you how much fun it really was. I know you'll get a laugh out of it.

For nearly a year before moving to Hawaii we negotiated for a place to meet for church. Just before we moved, those negotiations fell through, and our hopes went with them. After moving out of my home, surrendering my job, and travelling three weeks on the road, I got a call telling me the building deal was off.

My first reaction was anger, and then fear, that feeling of nausea that comes over you when things escape your control. Amplify that by the thought I might not have really heard God. The feelings were not only disruptive, they were terrifying. At this point I was anything but a model of faith.

The building deal really was off, and wasn't about to come back to life.

Aaron Suzuki and I flew over immediately and tried to round up other possibilities. One church said they might rent to us on Sunday evenings, but they changed their mind. Worse yet, they wrote us a rather nasty letter saying we should stay on the mainland. Hawaii had its fill of evangelicals in their eyes.

We got their letter an hour before we and our families boarded the plane for Honolulu. If that was a lousy send-off, the reception was no prettier.

We arrived to meet a hurricane warning and more rain than I had seen in the entire previous year. To make matters gloomier, I had rented a house in one of the rainiest areas of our island. Our shoes grew green mold just sitting in the closets.

If the rain was bad, the neighbors were grievous. Across the street lived two people with too much time on their hands. They kept themselves busy policing the neighborhood. They called the cops because they thought it was illegal to park a moving truck at the side of the road. Of course it was not, but they caused the hassle they intended.

They phoned the police again when my friend parked his rental car in front of my house overnight. That too is legal.

These lovely people struck gold when they complained about the Bible studies in our living room. The uniformed police were called twice, and a building inspector once. The problem was too many cars parked in front of one house. The harassment finally got to us and we moved the study.

I thank the Lord that I was also able to move my family after just two months of those "neighborly" people.

So much for the home front. The church started with 64 people meeting Sunday mornings under a tree in Kailua Beach Park. We had no permit, so we worried constantly about disruption from the authorities. We even faced the congregation away from the parking lot so people wouldn't see a possible approaching policeman. We figured that I could dismiss the service in an orderly manner while Aaron and Sonny stalled the officer.

Of course we really had no major problems. The previous difficulties weren't the fault of the police. They were always kind, and even apologized for being forced to respond to the calls. We were becoming overly fearful and simply didn't want to dismay our people any more than was necessary.

You should have seen the place! Beach chairs and boogie boards were piled everywhere. We brought tons of food, and ice chests abounded. It looked more like a company picnic than a church meeting. It had to. That was our disguise.

This church on the beach stuff may sound humorous, but it wasn't funny to us. Satan did his best to keep us from a legitimate meeting place. We found no pleasure in our circumstances at the time.

The last week on the beach it rained, and I was actually happy it did. People were beginning to like our really beautiful location. The beach was beautiful, but would have prevented growth and any sense of real order in our meetings. We had rented a building twelve miles away for the next Sunday. The rain really helped people feel thankful for the anticipated move.

The new location was a former restaurant at Heeia State Park. The park had a long history as a private park, and most recently the location had housed a tourist attraction called Ulu Mau Village.

A really great guy named Doug Mersberg managed the place. His board went to great lengths to convince the park system that it was legal to rent to a church.

We will be forever grateful to those people, as well as a man named Hugh Conser. Hugh is a member of a Honolulu church called Faith Fellowship and a real estate broker. Actually, he deals in the construction and sale of large shopping centers and industrial projects. Hugh spent three weeks combing Windward Oahu for rentable space. It was he who worked up the relationship with Heeia State Park. We believe he was a messenger from God sent especially to meet our need at that time.

We met at Heeia from October of 1983 through April of 1984 when we moved to Kapunahala Elementary School. Nice things happened at Kapunahala. The church immediately grew to over four hundred people. We had more space and we filled it. I also gained a wonderful friend in Jimmy Yoshimori, the principal. Jimmy introduced me to many people in the community and it was through his friendship that I finally stopped feeling like such an outsider to life in this community.

We celebrated our first anniversary with a huge luau. By that time, we had seen 500 people in church on a single Sunday. When we moved to Hawaii we had a five year goal of 450 and everyone we met thought we were crazy. As it turned out, we had sold short the Lord's ability to build His church. We also failed to grasp the great spiritual hunger in our community.

The first year brought many other wonderful surprises, especially people who have come to figure significantly in the ministry team.

Back when I was in Hermosa Beach, I had prayed for a Christian to build a surf shop. I knew what an influence good surfers have on the younger kids around them. The week we started church in Hawaii, Straight Up Surfboards opened for business. We didn't realize it at the time, but the guys who started the company were part of our church. God has used their love and open testimony of Jesus to turn many young hearts to the Lord.

Shannon Hill, who managed the company for three years, worked wonders in our youth program. He recently moved to Kona where he was appointed Youth Pastor at Hope Chapel. Surfing Magazine even did a small write up about his move. He was very effective building the shop, even more so in witnessing of Jesus.

Kaui Hill is Shannon's younger brother and the first in the family to find the Lord. He now pastors a MiniChurch as well as managing the surf shop. The whole family is involved in ministry, with their mother Jo and sister Kuuipo hosting MiniChurches in their homes.

Even the building where we lease office space proved a trailhead to blessing.

Aaron and I discovered an architect's office that would let us use their photocopy machine at a reasonable rate. The office manager was a young woman named Debra Tong; within a year she had joined our fellowship and became our office manager. Today, Debbie is my secretary. We thank God for the copy machine.

One day, in the elevator, I met a man who asked if we did marriage counseling. I told him we did, and invited him to church as well. He came to church with his wife and they gave their hearts to the Lord immediately. Their marriage got better due to mass infusions of God's word. I don't think they ever did make it in for the counseling. Rob and Debbie McWilliams joined my MiniChurch and moved on to help start Hope Chapel Leeward in Pearl City. Upon return from there, Rob took on the Men's Ministries in our church. He recently joined our pastoral team as a full-time member. You never know who you are going to meet in an elevator.

In the years that followed, growth has come steadily and there is a constant expectancy of the further blessing of God.

By our third anniversary we moved to Benjamin Parker Elementary School off Kamehameha Highway in Kaneohe. The move gave us larger facilities and the ability to park more cars. Ben Parker School is really the de facto community center for our side of the island. We feel very fortunate that the faculty is willing to share their building with us on weekends. Without their patience we would really face a huge problem. It is very difficult for a congregation our size to fit under a tree.

The church has grown to over eight hundred in weekly attendance. We have nearly twenty MiniChurches spread all over the island from Hawaii Kai to Makakilo. On a recent weekend more than a thousand people gathered for worship.

The MiniChurches are rapidly assuming the role of backbone in this church body. The maturing leaders are carrying an ever-growing load of ministry as they introduce the practical Word of God into people's lives.

MiniChurch has developed out of a "Bible study" mode. We enjoy a forum for discussing one's own life with regard to the message taught the previous Sunday. Wonderful changes occur when Christians seriously attempt to live what they believe. We are seeing less need for the hand-holding that goes on in the name of counseling, because our people are doing the Word rather than merely hearing it.

We find that healthy sheep create more sheep. This is true on the plane of personal evangelism but it also works at the level of church duplication. MiniChurch has become the breeding ground for leadership capable of planting exciting churches. This is much like what you read in the book of Acts. Our leaders are growing in the Lord and in the ability to shepherd His sheep. It is only natural that we have planted so many churches.

Our newest news is the birth of Hope Chapel Kahaluu, pastored by Kean Salzar with his wife Shelley. Started just before Easter they immediately grew from 125 to over 200. They are already training leadership for three daughter churches of their own.

The Lord blesses the discipleship process He initiated. We hope our new pastors can get some formal education after they get into ministry. However, we wouldn't trade all the seminary training in the world for eighteen months of on-the-job training as a MiniChurch pastor.

We still have no permanent location, although we are in negotiation for land so we can build. Land is scarce, therefore expensive. We have very limited financial resources and refuse to divert them from the task of building human lives. If we do build, and I absolutely expect we will, it will be because God has supplied our need. We cannot interrupt the function of the church for the sake of shelter.

You might pray for us as you read this. The need can only be met with God's help.

He brought us out of the nasty neighborhood, He rescued us from under the tree, and we know He has a permanent location large enough to house our growing church.

29

MOVING BY FAITH

I just heard a sad story.

Sadder still, it is an old story told over and over. You can change the names, but the essence is the same. In this case, it involves a complacent church. In the leader's words, "everything is under control." The problem is they are in control and have stopped growing.

When God calls the shots, there is usually some kind of growth. Often this growth is numerical progress as in a business that shows more profit, a church that brings more people to Christ or even a town where the population expands.

More often this growth takes place in the character or hearts of those who follow Jesus. Ideally, both take place at once.

In the case of this church, both types of growth have ceased. Everyone is sitting still having a good time, but they won't face real challenges. The worship is good, the fellowship so nice, and the finances are adequate. The difficulty is that everything is really nice. Too nice, if you ask me. If you aren't growing it is because you are dying.

When God is in control, there is always a challenge, always a risk. Sometimes it is frightening when He speaks, because He stretches us so far. When there is no risk there is no room for faith.

To grow we must be challenged, and those challenges must include the privilege of failing and yet still knowing the love of God.

A walk of faith is a walk of surrender to the Master. The Bible says, "We have the mind of Christ." My problem is that I also have a mind of my own. Too often I am unwilling to take the risks of obedience. I am too satisfied with a sure bet when God is calling me to step out in faith.

One of my favorite scriptures is Psalm 37 where we are told to delight ourselves in the Lord and He will give us the desires of our hearts. If we commit our way unto Him, He will bring those desires to reality.

I read that passage a couple of times every week and have done so for nearly thirty years. However, it was just a couple of weeks ago that I realized God is asking me to delight in His ways, in His will, so He can give me the desire of my heart. The rewards come in the context of His plan for my life.

This leads me to that Biblical list of men and women who overcame the world. I'm talking about those people in Hebrews chapter 11.

At first glance, these people are the framers of Old Testament history. A closer look shows that they only acted out someone else's plans. They lived lives of surrender to the Holy Spirit. The power in their lives resulted from their commitment to the Lord and His plans for them.

God is the architect of history and when we yield ourselves to Him, we really count for something. Our problem stems from our great ability at backseat driving. The men and women in Hebrews 11 left the driving to Him.

Abraham is the greatest example of a man leaving everything he knew and enjoyed, for a life in the unknown. God greatly blessed him for his choice and he became the role model of faith for us all.

For our discussion, perhaps Moses makes a better model. The Bible says, "By faith, Moses, when he had grown up, refused to be known as the son of Pharaoh's daughter. He chose to be mistreated along with the people of God rather than to enjoy the pleasures of sin for a short time."

What a choice! The man grew up in a palace and was certainly educated toward an important position in government. What made him think he had a better shot at improving the lot of the Israelis through personal activism than from a government job? It could only be the Spirit of the Lord.

Granted, he acted in the flesh on the day he beat up the Egyptian for God never gave him a license to kill. But it would be easy to fasten our eyes on the violence and fail to see that by intervention he marked himself as an Israeli. By getting involved, Moses chose to leave the Pharaoh's family and embrace his own people. The Spirit of the Lord was already at work in his heart.

Moses might have lived his life as some obscure government official in Egypt. With luck he may have even made some footnote on the pages of history. Almost certainly he would have remained rich and powerful. He intentionally gave up all the world offered for the uncertainty of following the Jehovah.

Moses is more than a footnote. He is the leader God chose for one of the most miraculous sequences of all time, the Exodus. He is also regarded as the father of most western legal codes. Beyond all that, if he were interested in power, playing number two to the Lord in the desert was pretty high up the chain of command.

If he had flinched for a moment on the day he rescued the Hebrew slave or had he refused God on the day the bush burned without consuming, he would have missed one of the greatest adventures of all time.

Moses never flinched! He surrendered at the right time to the proper Master and he never regretted it. Moses could have lived to lead his people into the promised land. His only big mistake came later when he struck the rock against God's command and that cost him dearly. He should have stuck to his guns and humbly obeyed the Lord. At the point that he asserted his own will he turned his back on the blessing God held for him.

I am writing all this to lead into a question....

What will you do when the Lord asks you to let go of the ring and give him the reins of your life?

I hope you will give Him everything He asks.

Moores and Suzukis arriving in Honolulu. Jane Koki is at
extreme left. Sonny Shimaoka is in center (1983).

Hope Chapel Windward begins at Kailua Beach Park (1983).

Hope Chapel Kaneohe office staff: Blaine Sato, Aaron Suzuki, Rob McWilliams, Debra Tong, John Honold, Jeff MacKay, Ralph Moore (1986).

Zac, Julie, and Michael Nazarian. The new pastor and his family (1984).

L-R: Julie Nazarian, Ruby Moore, Zac Nazarian, Ralph Moore at Hope Chapel Hermosa's twentieth anniversary.

Picture from 1983 Hope Chapel Hermosa calender.

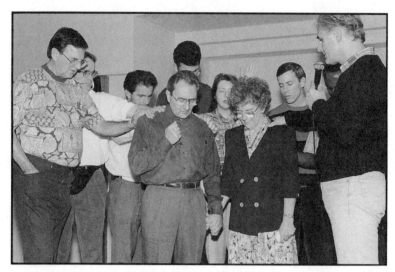

Council members and pastors commissioning Ken and Joan Capps for church-planting in England. L-R: Bob Lutman, Kurt Dahlin, John Shober, Clay Nestlerode, Meg Crowley, Greg Bray, Alan Kisaka, Ken and Joan Capps, Zac Nazarian.

Recently Acquired "Lucky" Market with Hope Hermosa tower rising in the background.

Ralph in Japan with Mrs. Yamasaki and Ross Yamauchi, who is now pioneering a church in Tokyo (1990).

A Minichurch in Hakodate, Japan. Pastor Ralph and Sonny Shimaoka with Pastor David Masui and Doctor Wataya. Wataya holds minichurch each Saturday morning for his pediatric staff (1989).

Moores at Christmas, 1991. Ralph, Kelly, Ruby, Carl.

A children's church baptism at Ben Parker school (1991).

30

ADDENDA 1992

This book is alive.

It is a continuing story of God at work in the lives of people who trust Him.

The story probably parallels that of any healthy church in the world. We know we have no lock on God's blessings.

Though it may not be unique, it is 'our' story, and my first priority is to write it for 'our' folks. I want every member of Hope Chapel to have a sense of the history of God's supernatural touch upon the life of our congregation. It is that touch that transforms ordinary sin-plagued people into active agents of God's love.

I realize that the vast majority who read these words won't be members of our church family. I'm trusting those readers to glean information helpful to their own circumstance.

I like to ask people to consider five attitudes of heart that they should possess before calling themselves members of our church.

I pause to list those conditions here before going on with the update to our story. My goal is to challenge you with a sense of ownership and assignment.

Ownership indicates that the heritage of your church belongs to you. It is a platform that God gave you for living life in community with other Christians. It also becomes a foundation for Christian service. Your church with all its strengths and weaknesses belongs to you. You should care for it in prayer and in service. You really own it.

Assignment suggests a calling: Did God place you in this congregation? If He did not, you should look elsewhere until you discover where you belong. If He did assign you to your church, you should actively seek a role of fruitfulness among these people.

This leads me to the five attitudes I mentioned earlier. You probably possess them all, but they are worth reviewing.

1. Do you love Jesus Christ and acknowledge Him as the Lord of your life and of this universe?

Many people come to a church for the fellowship or to meet someone of the opposite sex. I even met a man once who wanted to join our congregation for contacts to support his sales business. Is Jesus the Lord over your life as He is over the church?

2. Do you respect the church leaders and the direction they take?

Churches have a culture of their own. This culture is an expression of the personality of their people as they seek the Lord along with the personality and vision of the leadership. This culture is flavored by the special callings God puts upon each congregation.

Hope Chapel has a unique church culture. It shows in our dress and style of music. It's obvious in our emphasis on the needs of single adults and young families. You can't escape our calling to raise up pastors and plant churches. We spend lots of time addressing a revolution in thought when it comes to ministry in Japan. These things define us and make us different from other churches.

All of this is too much for some people. There are those who love the Sunday services but don't like our constant talk of Japan. Others prefer fancy buildings over a sacrificial mission to plant churches and care for people who hurt.

I remember the lady who constantly complained about the "rock strains" in our music. Every Sunday she would tell me, "I just love your teaching and the warmth of this church, but I may have to leave here because I can't stand that music." I'd just smile and listen to her complain week after week. Finally, I asked what she would do to the music if she could change it. In her answer, she described the music of at least fifty other churches on our island. I told her that I felt she ought to visit around. There are some pretty good preachers out there and most churches have music she likes.

Most church music is that of a generation ago and younger people don't have it in their hearts. We want to praise God with a true expression of our hearts. You don't ask Japanese speaking people to sing in English or you hamper their worship. You don't ask people of the eighties and nineties to sing the music of the forties or you hamper their worship.

We have a lot of "young people" with grey hair in our church. Some are in their seventies and early eighties. They feel comfortable with our worship because they would rather serve this generation than sing songs of their own past. I have extra respect for these folks and the love they bring to our church. They are with us because they know God's call in their life. They are willing to do things differently in order to accomplish the command our Lord gave us to preach the gospel to every person.

3. Are you willing to spend time with the church family?

Are these your people or do you limit your Christianity to a spectator function?

I believe you should develop at least one serious and solid friendship with another member of our church family. Now, I know you probably came to church with a friend in the first place. Eighty-seven per cent of our people came to this church through the love of a friend. What I ask is that you maintain that friendship and build others. You should involve yourself on a regular basis with those friends and make the Lord a part of your friendship.

This might happen in a MiniChurch or some other study group. It might mean involvement in an organized effort to feed the hungry or regularly visit someone in a convalescent home. You might just meet a friend for lunch on a regular basis. Or perhaps you'll disciple someone while you catch waves like I do once a week. My surfing has turned into a wonderful time of friends encouraging each other in the Lord.

You can't be fruitful if you try to live a Christian life outside the context of Christian relationships. Even the Lone Ranger had Tonto. You simply can't "go it alone."

The Bible tells us to "consider how we may spur one another on toward love and good deeds." How are we supposed to do that? "Let us not give up meeting together..." You have to spend time in a useful exchange with other Christians. Sunday meetings are great for learning and for worship but they fall short of allowing you to encourage one another in an exchange of love and friendship.

4. Do you believe in your church enough to stand with it financially?

I believe in tithing my income. My parents taught me to tithe (give ten per cent to the Lord) when I was just five years old. As a result, God has blessed and prospered my financial situation in so many ways that I can't take time to list them.

The rewards of taking God seriously over this have been many. In my life, job promotions and return on investments have gone way beyond my own wisdom and ability. I wholeheartedly suggest that you find out what God says about tithing.

However, whether you tithe or not isn't my real point here. The question I ask our people is, "Do you believe in this church enough to stand with us financially?"

Do you find integrity in this church? Can you trust the leadership?

Do you believe in the things we are doing?

Do you care enough to support the ministries that flow from this church like water from a spring?

Is this the principal place where your soul is fed?

If so, then this church should be the principal focus of your giving pattern. Many people align themselves with a local church but at the same time get enthralled with the color printing and glamour of some "media ministry." They attend the church and benefit from the ministry but focus their giving on some other organization because it seems large and successful.

You should support those who will stand over your grave and minister to your family when you are gone.

You should focus your giving on the ministry that is your first line of defense in your own struggle against Satan. This is why the Bible tells us to bring the tithe into the 'storehouse.' The storehouse in Old Testament days was a warehouse or granary from which the people were fed. The principle is as true today as it was when God spoke through the prophet Malachi. God wants us to invest in His spiritual granary "so there can be food in my house, says the Lord."

5. Are you willing to serve God?

I can't know what those words mean to you. Only God can speak to your heart and direct you into significant ministry.

Hope Chapel is a ministry team. The leaders are like coaches and the members are players on the field. The New Testament spells it out when it teaches that pastors and other leaders are placed in the church for "equipping the saints (that means every Christian) for the work of the ministry..."

God may call you to minister to your own family. He will probably call you to serve your immediate neighbors or perform some function within your own church. He may even call you to serve as a pastor or missionary. Rest assured he never calls us to do anything without making the task desirable. It really is fun serving God but it takes time and energy. Are you available?

Hope Chapel is simply people, loving God and each other. We promise to love people as they are, but we also promise to challenge them in their personal growth and relationship with Jesus Christ.

I hope you feel called to join a church family, be it ours or some other. The history, traditions, calling, and future of your church belong to you. You should develop a sense of ownership and a Godly pride in them. They are your spiritual heritage.

31

RAIDERS

Do you know the term 'wanna-be?'

It describes someone who "wants to be" something he isn't. There are wanna-be surfers at every beach and wanna-be stars at Hollywood parties and Beverly Hills gas stations.

On autumn Monday nights there are millions of wanna-be football coaches and general managers glued to their television screens. I am one of those.

Al Davis is general manager of the Los Angeles Raiders. His team has the best win-loss record of any team in professional sports. He coached the team at one time and was commissioner of the old American Football League. He has three Super Bowl rings. In 1992, he was inducted into the Professional Football Hall of Fame. If I could be in football, I would want to perform like Mr. Davis. I'm not in football, but I still want to be like this man.

He always gets the best performance out of his players and coaches. He takes players who can't get along on other teams or who seem to have aged beyond their potential and turns them into an important part of a winning team.

Whether it's Lyle Alzado, Jim Plunkett, or Ronnie Lott, Al Davis picks up players who were rejected and gives them another chance. His success is as a developer of other people's potential.

I've never met Mr. Davis and don't know if he is a Christian, but he is one of my heroes.

Churches often become societies of the self-righteous. I want our church to function as a team of second chances.

Jesus went into the world and chose some apparent losers. He called them to Himself and forged a team that today comprises nearly a third of the population of the planet. It would probably be larger if we remembered that He sent us to the lost and dying, the poor and broken rather than the rich and well put together.

The Christian church exists to offer second chances.

This is true at conversion. God promises to love us in spite of our sin and failure. But what about the leadership team? It is often the misfit who is capable of the greatest creativity and is motivated to the greatest love. Jesus said that he who had the most forgiven would love the most.

A good example is Jeff MacKay. Jeff started a church three years ago in a community on Oahu called Mililani. The church began with a handful of high school students and today numbers over five hundred people. Jeff recently married Naoko who comes from Japan. Through her God is opening new doors for him to minister in that country as well.

I met Jeff several years ago in Hermosa Beach. He was working his way through L.I.F.E. Bible College by running our church printing press.

In those days he didn't look too promising. With his blond hair falling in his face and his wire-rimmed glasses sliding down his nose coupled with mild dyslexia didn't pose him as "most likely to succeed."

Jeff is pretty artistic and like many artists, he's not terribly organized. In fact, I fired him from our print shop for sloppy work. That was shortly before I moved to Hawaii and you can imagine my surprise when he asked if he could come with us as part of the ministry team. He had just graduated and wanted to pursue the pastorate.

I said that he could come but he would have to get a secular job and work in the church as a volunteer. You guessed it. He got a job in a print shop.

I asked Jeff if he would start a Bible study with our junior high kids. He jumped in and very quickly had forty students. He kept getting into trouble with parents for keeping their children out too late, but the kids were growing in the Lord. But one Saturday he took a bunch of kids hiking over a broken suspension bridge across a deep gulch. When the parents heard about it, I had to remove him from the youth group. In other words, he got fired again.

Jeff's response? He started a high school group (he figured those parents wouldn't stress out so much if the kids stayed out late).

Within a couple of months there were over seventy high schoolers attending the Bible study groups he started!

Jeff was forever overspending his budget and we often had to bail him out of trouble with parents, but ministry was happening! Kids got saved and lives were changed! A natural evangelist, Jeff told people about the Lord everywhere he went, even in Japan when he couldn't speak Japanese: he would pantomime, draw pictures, or use a dictionary. He did whatever it took to introduce people to the Lord.

One day he shared the Lord with a high school girl from Mililani after surfing. She spread the word to her friends, and they started a Bible study. Someone from another Hope Chapel taught the study for a while but felt ill- prepared for the large numbers involved. Parents even got involved and it became apparent that a church was trying to come to life. Those people recruited Jeff and today he pastors a strong church that gives spiritual leadership to the entire community. They number more than 500 in attendance.

The most powerful management book of the 1980's was Tom Peters' "In Search of Excellence." It is a manual for successful business and service organizations. I've read it five times and each time I do, I'm struck all over again with his concept of a mentor or 'champion.' Peters would see the Apostle Paul as more than a teacher to Timothy or Barnabas to John Mark. He describes the need for the older man to train, role model, and protect the younger leader. Part of equipping the saints for ministry includes protecting them while they make their mistakes.

I find that this is a great and rewarding part of my job as pastor and equipper. I am constantly challenged to work with failure in those I train. Everyone who succeeds fails at one time or another.

The difference between real success and failure is learning from your mistakes and getting lots of chances to swing the bat. During his baseball career, Reggie Jackson struck out more times than any batter in history. He also broke just about every batting record around. You have to take chances with people or you produce nothing.

The lesson of Jeff MacKay was one for me, not him. If I try to protect my own reputation (hang on to that ring of control), I will miss out on men like Jeff.

There were plenty of times that I wanted to give up on Jeff because I worried about what others might think of me or of the church due to his behavior. Today, I am proud of what they think of us due to Jeff's great accomplishments. If my fears had won, our ministry would be a lot smaller than it is today. Jesus spoke of this when He said you must lay down your life (including reputation) for His sake if you really want to find it. He also said that if you try to hold on to your life, you will lose it. The challenge for me continues: "Can I see people through the Lord's eyes and cooperate with his plan for their lives? Or will I worry about safely getting through life with a limited amount of trouble?"

I know I'll continue to watch Monday Night Football as a frustrated "armchair coach." But Jesus puts the same kinds of decisions in my lap every week when it comes to the 'players' on our team. I've learned a lot from Al Davis and others, but the biggest risk-taker and giver of second chances is still the Holy Spirit.

One of the most challenging things I have encountered here in laid-back Hawaii is the culture. It is always a challenge to get someone who is born and raised here in Hawaii to get more involved in leadership. I have been accused lately of being racially prejudiced against Caucasians or "haoles" as they are called here, but I recognize a need to equip the saints that live here to do the works of the ministry so that we can have a real effect upon the local populace and not just the people who move here to Hawaii from the Mainland. The local guy seems to want to just "hang loose" while the mainland haole is raring to go. But the truth is that the local guy is just a little more afraid of making a mistake. The local culture here has lots of Oriental influence and the notion of "saving face" keeps many guys from trying for fear of failure and "losing face." We just have to find ways to build up these guys and keep them trying!

The other extreme is the local guy who is driven by success. I have a couple of these guys in my church right now: John Honold, who runs our high school ministries and our worship, and Corey Grinder, who used to take care of our singles and overseas ministries.

John came to us as a former nightclub singer. I tried to use him as a worship leader, but had to sit him down for a whole year because I felt that he was drawing more attention to himself than to God in his worship leading. He sat for a year, faithfully doing whatever he could to help, and when he came back, he showed that he had learned something. John helped to start our singles ministries and now runs our Youth Dept. which is beginning to provoke more ministry among the youth in the state of Hawaii amongst a number of churches and schools.

I had heard about Corey from my secretary Debra. He had shared the Lord with Deb a couple of years before she ended up in our church. Corey had a reputation as someone who couldn't stay put, and had a difficult time submitting to leadership. When he came to Hope, after preaching in the Hawaiian language and doing ministry for another church, I made him sit for 6 months under a couple of my youth pastors. He could give kids rides to a high school MiniChurch, nothing else. He stuck it out and eventually became our Singles Pastor and Director of Overseas Ministries.

John and Corey have disagreements. They both have very strong personalities. But they have bought into our values here at Hope and have become "Raiders." Their presence in our church has helped us to have a solid impact upon the local community here on Oahu.

32

TEAM-BUILDING

Culture is an important part of life.

Tourists come to Hawaii to enjoy the culture as well as the climate.

But the culture they pursue is often a fantasized memorial to the past. Real cultural differences are not so romantic and are often unnoticed.

The 1990's bring disturbing recurrences of racism to the American cultural fabric. Hopefully, Hawaii will dodge some of that. Our cultural mosaic has long been many colored and most recently, a picture of harmony.

The Christian church in our state reflects the cultural variation of the population, with one exception. The haoles (caucasians) tend to dominate church leadership circles. The reason for that is cultural. Haoles are culturally more aggressive and tend to volunteer quickly. Local people are taught to hold back until asked. It is not too polite to offer yourself for a job and may even be considered prideful in many circles.

Our usual approach to recruitment is to hold off the haoles from the mainland till we have time to speak with people who reflect the culture and heritage of our community. One of our stated missions for this church is to raise up more local people as pastors and leaders.

Sometimes I get called a racist because I am more interested in working with people with black hair than with blondes. The truth is, I am interested in balancing the leadership structure of the Christian community. Hawaii is peopled by twenty three per cent caucasians. The rest of the people have black hair and brown skin. It only makes sense to work hard at developing leaders who can minister to the majority. Too often, local people are 'put off' because the cultures doesn't match for good communication.

Another problem in Hawaii is the practice of recruiting pastors from the mainland which often overlooks local people who are equally well trained and culturally better adapted to the job. We want to reverse these trends in our church and the rest of the state.

I recognize a need to equip the saints that live here to do the works of the ministry so that we can have a real effect upon the local populace and not just the people who move here from someplace else.

For that reason, we carefully balance our recruiting efforts to include all our people. The result is a church comprised of and led by local people. We have haoles, too (I'm a proof of that), but our church is operated by the people who populate our community. Coupled with our "on the job" approach to training the ministry, this results in a church staff and pioneer pastors who reflect the heritage of our community. We believe this is one of our real strengths.

Very often the problem is getting the local person to take a chance or be willing to stand up and declare themselves capable of a task. Many well-qualified people hold back for fear others will think them prideful. Some were taught, as children, that they are country people and incapable of leadership roles.

In the midst of this struggle I ran into two local guys that think and act just the opposite of the scenario I am describing. These guys were driven by success.

You met John Honold in an earlier chapter. His high school counterpart and arch-competitor was Corey Grinder. Both are half-Japanese and half-Caucasian.

In their 'pre-Christian' days, these guys played football against one another, modeled clothing for the same department store, and dated some of the same girls. They also didn't like each other very much. Ten years later, both served on our pastoral staff.

They brought an unhealthy rivalry into our team. The Bible tells us that 'promotion' comes from the Lord. He lifts one up and pulls another down. Any time competition for recognition enters into ministry, it is the work of Satan and never the Holy Spirit.

I won't go into the struggles between these two men, but they were an adventure for the rest of us. They finally came to a real peace between themselves. At times, we all wished they would take their competition elsewhere. But we knew it was impossible. God marked them both for ministry and He placed them on our staff. John came so obviously delivered to us by the Lord, and it was John who brought Corey on staff. Yet they couldn't get along.

As I write this chapter, Corey is in Japan having just assumed the pastorate of a broken congregation. John is laying plans to pioneer a church in west Oahu. These men are real 'heroes' when it comes to ministry. Both are extremely well-liked and very productive at discipling others. With raw-boned submission to God, they struggled to get along for five years and really made peace just months before they were separated by thousands of miles of ocean. Neither could go on to full potential without the love they finally attained.

Why do I bring all this up in a book designed to tell about the good times and blessings of the Lord? Because the hard times are the good times and the struggles reveal His blessing. God is building people and He often builds the biggest people out of those with the biggest ego problems. Letting go of the ring has to include giving Him time to iron out the wrinkles in those around us.

Again, He is the God of second chances.

33

BUILDING BRIDGES

Six years ago, we sent a team of four young men to Japan for a summer outreach.

They brought one young boy to the Lord. He brought along fourteen of his friends.

Within six months those boys brought enough excitement home that the total number of new people in the church was forty five. Their parents were coming to church. Six months after that, only the first boy and his father were walking with the Lord. The boy eventually fell away.

The boys belonged to a kind of a street gang. When the first of them ran away from home he came to the church where my friends were staying because his dad knew the pastor. The dad is the only person left out of what seemed like a revival....

Why did the others fall away?

It seems that the culture of that church was too isolated from the culture of non-Christian Japanese people. Americans have a heavy influence upon church songs and traditions in Japan. That influence often renders the church too 'un-Japanese' for most people to feel comfortable.

In the situation I just described, only the man who already knew the pastor remained with the church. He was the only person with a built-in 'bridge' into the life of that congregation.

That bridge allowed him to overcome the 'foreignness' of the church environment. He stuck with it long enough to learn the necessary Christian vocabulary, music tastes and behavior code that would allow him to participate in the church.

Studies show that people like to worship God in the presence of those they know and trust. They also prefer to worship with people with tastes similar to their own.

The reason some churches grow and others do not is their ability to help people describe the Lord to their close friends in ways that are friendly and familiar. People respond to love and they respond to familiar styles of music, dress, communication, and even architecture.

In our own church, eighty-seven percent of the people came through the invitation of a friend and sixty-five percent of our people got saved through the ministry of someone in our own church. This suggests that we are 'packaging' the gospel in terms familiar with our generation and culture.

The burden to adapt is on the person with the message rather than on the listener.

Paul circumcised Timothy in order to maintain an audience with Jewish people living in Jerusalem. He had to adapt to the cultural demands of his audience. In the same way, I had to adapt to reach hippies back in California and then change again when those hippies turned to yippies. My whole approach to life changed drastically when I moved to

Hawaii. I had to change in order to understand and communicate with the people I wanted to reach.

Lately, I'm learning to speak Japanese. Along with it I'm learning some surprising things about Japanese people.

Japan is changing rapidly.

Every newspaper you read has at least one article about social change in that country. The change upsets many people, but it is opening new doors for the gospel.

The younger people in Japan are often called 'Shinjinrui.' The term ties together the Japanese written characters for three separate words. They are new, man, and kind. New-man-kind. The suggestion is of a generation out of control. They have vastly different views from their parents on most issues.

This is a relatively new phenomenon in Japan. For generations, people have simply adopted the values and traditions of their elders. The Japanese national proverb is, "the nail that stands up will be driven down." It means that you don't dare stand out in a crowd. The overwhelming need to conform defined society for many generations. Young kids in blue jeans are "driving down" the ancient proverb and the society it defined.

Economic shock and a new position in the world structures of power and politics drastically affect the man on the street.

People and values are changing. Young people are more likely to identify with a British rock group than with the music and poetry of Japan. Clothing styles are European and every Japanese car manufacturer has a design studio in Los Angeles in an attempt to monitor the latest in California thinking. The latest fad involves young people imitating Afro-American athletes and entertainers. They go to the extreme of painting their faces black and wearing clothes that replicate those of their current idol.

These 'new-people' think different than any generation that has gone before. They display values little understood by their elders. Without hope of home ownership, they spend conspicuously on cars, clothes, and entertainment. They desire free time above job promotion or security.

They carry with them a new set of social problems as well. Violent crime and scandals over cheating on school admissions tests outrage the whole country.

The recent Recruit Scandal and the admission that brokerage firms covered the losses of their biggest clients during the Nikkei run-up have made cynics of many young people. New revelations of yakuza, Japanese Mafias, and their octopus tentacles reaching into legitimate business and government haven't helped the young embrace the values of their elders.

The price tag for decades of prosperity is an erosion of social values. As traditional and post-war values recede, so does the mortar that holds this nation together. The soul of Japan is "up for grabs."

Freedom of movement, money for luxuries, free time, and "marriage for love" are characteristics of this generation. Gone are long hours at the office, formal dress and speech, arranged marriages, and scrimping for the future. These people are also spiritually hungry.

New Age religions sweep the country as people replace the materialism of the post-war years with a craving for life in the inner man. It is very easy to bring younger people to a knowledge of the Lord. The problems start when you try to introduce them to church. The churches are traditional and closed to outsiders. This is why the average attendance in Japanese churches is 38 people. It also explains why there are twice as many Christians as there are church attenders in Japan. A recent survey by the Japan Broadcasting Corporation (NHK) shows that the number who claim to be Christians is close to 2% while attendance tallies come in at less than 1%. Many non-attenders are younger people or those who found Christ while studying abroad. To most of them, Japanese churches are unfriendly, too traditional, and irrelevant to their personal needs.

One friend of mine recently returned to Japan after becoming a Christian in our church. She tried three churches but could find no church that seemed loving. I asked Christians from one of the churches she visited about how accepting their church was. They lectured me on how important it is to "examine new people carefully to see if they really fit into our church or not."

This attitude is far removed from Jesus' admonition to go to the highways and bring them in. Churches are often judgmental and more reminiscent of the Pharisees than of the early Christians. The Christian church ought to be the most loving and accepting group of people in Japan.

The future looks hopeful. The advent of social change carries with it real possibilities for the emergence of new leaders who possess freedom from the past and its snare of tradition.

The worldwide church growth movement is beginning to impact Japanese Christian institutions. Because of this new thrust, young church leaders now compare church and denominational traditions to Scripture and ask, "Why are we doing things this way?"

We now face the real possibility of church culture changing to match the changes occurring in the streets and coffee shops all over Japan. Younger pastors ponder principles learned from church growth teachers and leaders. These ideas include target marketing and cultural accommodation while clinging to an unchanging message. Some are actually planning churches tailored specifically to the needs of the young. Churches that have already done this are growing rapidly and other pastors are taking note. The success of one man breeds courage in another.

We should pray for grassroots leadership that can take advantage of these changes and embrace the future. We need leaders who can address a society that claims the Bible as its best-selling book and is building Christian wedding chapels into all of its major hotels. Japan is hungry, and the interest in Christianity is high. Interest in church, as currently presented, is low. If we change our approach, the much anticipated and often prophesied revival may soon break out.

God is opening doors and building bridges between our church and Japan. The purpose is to help Japanese Christians build bridges between themselves and the non-Christians around them.

Our goal is to start 'Shinjinrui' churches.

Jesus told us that you cannot put new wine into old wineskins without breaking the skins. He spoke of leather wine bottles that could no longer stretch to accommodate the expansion that accompanies fermenting wine. The comparison is obvious. Older churches have their own tradition and heritage. It would invite disaster to fill them with the fresh work of the Spirit in a new generation.

The older congregations are filled with faithful people and you would never want to destroy them. For this reason we hope to see hundreds, perhaps thousands of new churches in Japan during the coming years. Those churches must be peopled and led by 'Shinjinrui.'

We've worked for several years to gain the necessary understanding and earn the privilege of starting churches in Japan. We didn't think we could just march in and "do our stuff." Others have labored long and hard in the harvest of Japan. We needed to learn much and are still learning as we begin pioneering some of the churches we believe God is calling into existence.

Our summer teams have built friendships from Hokkaido to Okinawa for six years. Eight people from those teams have moved back to Japan for longer term ministry.

Debra Fairbairn, Laura Iwamoto, Rohnda Pintor, Anna Simao and Jamie Olsen taught English as an avenue of making friends and sharing the gospel. Ross Yamauchi and Sean Odani moved to Japan to assist in churches and started churches in Tokyo and Yokohama. Corey Grinder and his wife Lisa just assumed the pastorate of a lovely congregation in Tokorozawa. Clinton Landeza is in Okinawa where he began a youth ministry among students who are struggling to fit into their own society.

All these people exhibit a Christianity that is grace-oriented and exciting to their friends in Japan. Their lives demonstrate love that is attractive to non-Christians. This love easily bridges that gap between the church and the world.

People from the summer teams started a new ministry in Hawaii three years ago. They called it 'Bridge.' The idea was to bring younger Japanese Christians to our church with a mind to demonstrate worship forms and church tradition that could reach other young people. In fact, we were asked to do this by a very forward thinking Japanese pastor, Seita 'David' Masui.

We have quite a number of Japanese students in our service each Friday evening. They seem to like the casual dress and 'rock' sound of the worship music. We've been told this would be offensive to Japanese Christians, but this is their favorite among our services. These students actually gave David the idea for Bridge. If they enjoyed our church, why not teach others in Japan to borrow some of what we were doing?

Bridge is a three week intensive study in God's grace, apologetics, New Testament values, tourism, and fun. It is also responsible for at least two marriages with a couple more on the horizon. The exciting results are several churches coming to life in Japan. Also, a couple of brand new churches sent people to Bridge during their foundational stages. Both are growing very rapidly. Kobe Bible Fellowship is attracting nearly one hundred people each week and is less than two years old. Osaka Bible Fellowship is just three months old and numbers more than forty people. These numbers are very significant if you remember that the average church attendance in Japan is only thirty eight people.

One of my best friends is Steve Fox, a half-Japanese who was once a 'rock star' in Japan. Today, he is an Assembly of God missionary. We were both trained and discipled by the same man, Robert Houlihan, when we were young. Steve teaches us much about Japan and its culture. His friendship is a gift from God, and his ministry in Japan is linking together many people whose new ideas are beginning to make a big difference.

Our newest staff member is Junji Ono. He translates books into Japanese and for years we were friends when he translated for me when I spoke in Japan. Junji now oversees all our efforts at ministry in Japan.

Junji, Steve, and Yo Masui started a new Japanese language church in Honolulu last year. Their target audience are mostly Shinjinrui living in our country. They call it Bridge of Hope.

Through men like these and the many wonderful friends we have on the other side of the ocean, God is building some wonderful bridges to people possessing great spiritual hunger.

We are trusting God to use us in some small way to help stir up the tidal wave of revival so necessary to the future of Japanese Christianity.

Pray for us!

34

TAKING THE LAND

In 1988, our church council felt we should pursue land for a church building.

The first plan was to build a chapel for a nearby college. We would use the facility on weekends, they could have it during the week.

It seemed like a great idea, but they wanted a gym instead of a chapel. Besides, we are a very active church and would need offices and some classroom space throughout the week.

Plan two was to build a strong savings account or "building fund." We had no land or visibility of land, yet we would begin saving by faith. By that I mean faith that God would provide land for sale.

At the time it seemed pretty naive. We 'knew' there was no land available in Kaneohe. We had searched tax maps and approached several owners to no avail.

During the spring, we sought God and presented the possibilities of moving by faith to the congregation. A group of concerned people put together a project called "Faith For The Future." We would present the need for land and building to the congregation in the most complete and detailed way possible. We knew that people would give if they understood the need and the potential. Our church is generous and love to give when it produces ministry.

We spent the whole spring communicating the need for a church building and asking people to pray. We wanted them to ask God what He would challenge them to give above their normal tithes and offerings. We used a slogan to communicate this, "A God-inspired sacrifice, a God-supplied gift." We would trust the Lord to challenge us to give beyond our comfort zone (God-inspired sacrifice) and then to supply the amount He specified (God-supplied gift).

The church responded wonderfully.

At a banquet in the Ilikai Hotel, we held a night of praise and worship and collected "commitment cards," pledging financial gifts toward the building fund. Nearly every person in the church showed up. It was a night of reverence and wonder just to experience the love in that room. At the end of the evening, people promised nearly nine hundred thousand dollars toward the building.

That was in May. By September God supplied land for the project.

I arrived in my office one morning to find a real estate listing on my desk. Someone was offering to sell us a 54-year lease to nine acres of land on the side of a mountain overlooking Kaneohe town and bay. I was really shocked. We had approached many landowners, asking them to sell. People never came asking us to buy.

God was at work. He challenged our faith and then acted in response to it. As soon as we began to save for it, He provided land.

By January of 1989 we obtained the right to use that land for the next two generations. Everyone accelerated their giving and the land became ours. The cost, just $300,000. It's a lease and we hope to purchase it in the distant future, but for now it is ours and we got it at a price we could certainly afford. God's timing of the fund raising campaign and the offer to lease couldn't have been more precise.

As I write these words, we have drawings for our new church home and are about to enter into a process called "site plan review" with the city of Honolulu. We face monstrous drainage problems created by the construction of a freeway on the mountain above us. Our immediate neighbors, a housing development on the hill below us are not too excited about our congregation driving on the roads we share. We have about $600,000 in the bank and the project will cost five million. You could say our backs are against the wall, or you could say we stand to see God doing the miraculous in the near future.

I'll go with God. He has come through so many times in the past. The future looks bright from where I sit.

When the building is completed it will be located on the highest physical elevation in Kaneohe. The view is astounding. You can see the whole bay and much of the Windward Coast on one side. You view Kailua and the Pali from the other. More important, it will provide us with a secure home base for ministry.

We need a place where we can leave equipment set up from day to day and week to week. We need the freedom of schedule our own place will afford. We need to know that the state won't ask us to leave as they do from the school where we meet a couple of Friday nights and one Sunday morning each year. We need freedom from the threat that the school could be taken away and we would have to disband Hope Chapel.

Giving to the project remains important, yet prayer is more important. The Bible says, "You have not because you ask not." We are asking and we expect the Lord to send the answers we seriously need. He will come through.

In the meantime, I've noticed the blessing of God during the waiting process.

Just as the nation of Israel grew to maturity during the time in the wilderness, we are becoming strong as we wait for our own home.

The emphasis must remain on people, never buildings or stained glass. I like it that way. If we could be guaranteed the use of the school forever, I would opt for that. The school keeps us humble and provides a safety against the architectural pride that afflicts churches.

While operating without a building, we've enjoyed giving birth to twenty-two daughter and granddaughter churches. In addition to those mentioned previously, there are many wonderful new churches. Hope Chapel Kahalu'u was pioneered by Kean Salzer. Jim Phillips pastors Hope Chapel Hawaii Kai along with an exciting youth team made up of Gordon Horne, a chaplain at Kamehameha Schools, and Tony Moniz, a professional surfer. Chuck Klingman pastors My Father's House in Manoa and Kelly Hildebrand pastors a Hope Chapel in nearby Mo'ili'ili. Jeff MacKay is in Mililani and John Haag has assumed the pastorate of Hope Chapel Leeward while Stephen Laudise became pastor of Hope Chapel Kailua.

On the Big Island, Hope Chapel Kona gave birth once again to Hope Chapel Ka'u where Nick Sokach is pastor.

During the past few months I've become good friends with Wayne Cordiero of New Hope Christian Fellowship and that has drawn us much closer to their churches in

Waimea where Larry Gillis pastors and to New Hope in Puna planted by Alex Pacheco. Of course, we did nothing in regard to starting those three churches, but God has bound our hearts together with the same vision for Hawaii and Japan. New Hope churches are reaching a vast percentage of the population in East Hawaii and we have much to learn from them.

On Kauai we were involved with the resurrection of The Sanctuary, a church that was in the throes of death. The pastor who brought new life is Bob Burton. He was instrumental in giving birth to Lighthouse Christian Church in Kilauea where John Schmelling pastors. Bob is currently working with LeRoy Metzler to start Hope Chapel South Shore in Poipu.

While most are in Hawaii, there is also a new church in Vancouver, British Columbia begun by Curtis Blanchet and Andrew Lum. Ken Ogawa is building a pioneer congregation in West Los Angeles.

We are involved with the new churches in Japan mentioned in the previous chapter, and the future there looks bright with the possibility of many more churches attuned to the needs of a younger generation.

Our MiniChurches now total more than sixty.

The pastoral staff has grown to eleven people. Gisele Ferriera left a job as a court reporter to direct our Children's Church. She just had a baby and gave that job to Lisa Lum. Kaala Souza left a surf shop and coaching job in a high school to become Junior High Pastor. Allan Lau interrupted a teaching career and is our new Singles Pastor. Junji Ono moved from Japan and is Missions Coordinator. Mark Hsi runs a successful construction company while doubling as a volunteer in charge of Counseling Ministries. To keep us all together Wendell Elento, a graduate of the United States Naval Academy, left a shipboard career and currently manages our entire staff. Add to these a legion of clerical staff and over eight hundred volunteers, and you have a church that concentrates on people.

We are blessed by our circumstances, building or no building.

The new building should be complete by 1994. When it is finished, we will have a much-needed tool for housing the ministry and launching many more churches. Meanwhile, character development and maturity are God's plan for the present. Expanded ministry is His goal for our future.

35

FAMILY

This is the "Year of the Family."

Hollow words to cover the pain of broken families. The United States has more hurting families than any other developed country.

We declared God dead in the sixties. We embraced "sex, drugs and rock 'n' roll" in the seventies. Money was king during the Ronald Reagan eighties. Youth gangs and racial hatred are the agenda for the nineties. Families died when Americans threw God away.

Unless God does something wonderful, the American family will be an institution of the past. Yet we hope for miracles. Revivals turn cultures around. God is at work in our church and thousands of others. He said He would place the homeless into families. That starts with a healthy church family that knows how to reach out in love.

All the counseling in the world adds up to nothing without sustaining love from people nearby. Our church exists to train people for ministry. More simply put, we are here to teach people to love those who hurt with God's redeeming and accepting love.

We hope to raise up an army to love the unlovely. The task is painful and often difficult, but very simple. An old song says it, "...with one hand reach out to Jesus, with the other bring a friend."

The message of a God who forgives made personal, through people who know how to love, will heal the heart of our nation.

Will you be that friend? It involves a surrender of time, energy and that "ring of control." It will cost you much but you will find the adventure indescribable.

It was Jesus who said, "For whoever wants to save his life will lose it, but whoever loses his life for Me and the gospel will save it." Allow Him the driver's seat and life becomes really worth living.

36

GIVE 'EM HEAVEN

Nothing's cooled off in Hermosa Beach.

The church is healthy and touching thousands of people through its many outreaches.

Early in his ministry, Zac ended a service with a little different charge to the congregation. He said, "Too many people are giving each other hell all week. You go out there and give 'em heaven."

The words caught fire in the hearts of the people. "Give 'em heaven!" became the rallying cry of a church bent on serving others.

The result is ministry far beyond what I could have imagined back in 1971, when I started the church. Truth is, no one would have expected this much fruit when I left for Hawaii in 1983.

Let me give you some numbers.

In 1991, the leaders set a goal to hand out 1 million gospel tracts: the congregation gave away 1.3 million. The church fed 4,913 hungry people through its "Hope in Action" ministry. At Christmas, 600 adults ministered to more than 200 children of prisoners in the Los Angeles County Jails.

They continue to plant churches. As a result, more than 20 new congregations exist that did not in 1983 when I left for Hawaii.

Even before the L.A. riots, Zac began strategizing to plant churches in the inner city. He is working with Dr. Paul Hackett, who pastors Crenshaw Imperial Foursquare Church, and several other pastors. They believe that only the gospel provides the compassion and hope needed to heal a wounded community.

The recent rioting brought many other congregations into a network that offers a foundation for future ministry. Churches have shown themselves compassionate through financial commitments to feed people while the city is rebuilding. The hope is that the coalition formed in this stressful time will continue to bear fruit for a long time. Love and understanding will bridge the gap of injustice. Food and money are just the beginning.

"Hope for Life" provided the largest representation at the Southern California Life Chain, with over 1000 volunteers from the church attending the Pro Life demonstration.

The Hope Academy now boasts 65 families and more than 100 children in a well-organized home schooling effort. These kids get together for field trips, as well as technical and musical training.

Vision for ministry overseas is exploding. In 1991 alone, 120 people took vacation time to travel internationally on church-sponsored missions. Teams traveled to India, Africa, the Philippines, Romania, Ecuador, and Belize. Closer to home, people have made countless trips into Mexico to feed the poor and share the gospel.

The Romanian ministry was dramatic because of the hunger for God found in the oppressed people of that nation. The team didn't get to set up shop before all their Bibles were gone. Local people pitched in while they were unloading boxes of Bibles from the van at the first distribution point. By the time the Bibles were unloaded, they were all given away to people desperate for the Word of God.

The Belize team was a scouting party for a new church. Newlyweds Jimi and Julaine Calhoun are planting a new church in Belize. Jimi left the pastorate of Hope Chapel in Sherman Oaks, California, which he started four years ago. Belize marks his second round as a pioneer pastor.

Jimi has an interesting history. He enjoyed fame and made a lot of money as a member of the Jimi Hendrix Band in the seventies. A couple of years after he turned to the Lord, he set it all aside asking for a job as a janitor in the Hermosa church so he could spend time hanging around the pastors learning the ministry. After several years of discipleship, he left Hermosa Beach and started the ministry in Sherman Oaks. Now he's off to Belize. It's a pretty long way from the spotlights of huge rock concerts to this small nation on the north coast of South America. Jimmy is a tenacious, faithful man. He will do well.

Hope Chapel Hermosa is now debt-free. They paid off their last mortgage in early 1992, but haven't yet built their new church facility.

In 1987, they purchased the Lucky Market next door to the church. They bought it for a couple of million dollars from an insurance company. We are talking about a supermarket with acres of parking and a spectacular view of the Pacific Ocean. The reason for the wonderful price is that the property is under lease to Lucky until the year 2007.

In February 1992, Zac sent a letter to the entire church asking them to stop sending money to the building fund. The bowling alley-turned-church, the supermarket for future development, and three houses for a parking lot are all debt-free. Nearly one and a half million dollars sits in the bank, waiting to transform the market into a church auditorium. There is simply no need for more money. This reminds me of Moses asking the people to stop giving to the tabernacle construction in Exodus 35 and 36.

The great need, of course, is to buy out the lease and remodel the market into badly needed church facilities. Only the Lord knows when that will happen. In the meantime, I'm proud of Zac and company for having the integrity to turn away funds. They are helping restore credibility that Christianity has lost in the past few years.

The congregation currently rents the Hermosa Beach Community Center for one of its six services each weekend. Zac shuttles between services, preaching in one location while people are worshipping in the other. The schedule is grueling, but effective.

As you read this, please pray for an equitable resolution of the logjam presented by the lease. The market is sitting on a six hundred dollar a month lease that they have held since 1956. The market hardly wants to move with rent like that. I believe God has a solution that is good for the market, the church, and the community.

We should always remember that a church is people, never a building.

The New Testament says we are like bricks or "living stones" built into a spiritual temple for the Lord. If we are the stones, then love and commitment are the mortar. The church exists to train its members for acts of ministry to one another and the world.

The Hermosa church is doing a great job at this training process. That job is evidenced by the numbers we looked at earlier. But let me tell you some of the exciting things they are doing in order to train others.

They now have three levels of "Roots" training for new Christians. Nine hundred people went through those classes in 1991.

The church now offers a series of one day seminars for aspiring MiniChurch pastors. MiniChurch pastors are getting much more hands-on training as they care for their own people. The whole church has been pretty much restructured around the MiniChurch concept. This allows for a much larger ministry and pastoral care team, as well as the training opportunity that produces churches in other localities. The great exodus to lower cost housing in Orange and San Diego counties brought an attrition of MiniChurch pastors, but many new people are rising up to take their place.

The Hope Chapel Ministries Institute enrolled 825 people in classes during 1991, and many of those are MiniChurch pastors hoping to go on and plant a new church in the future.

The entire church recently read through the Daily Bible together for the second year in a row. People are interested in the Scriptures for the power they give to live a godly life. These people are committed to bring light into their world. They really live like salt in the earth.

Since I left in 1983, they haven't missed a beat. The original vision that God gave a bunch of young hippies back in 1971 continues to bear fruit well into the nineties.

We can only expect that kind of fruit where people sincerely walk in faith and abide in Christ.

By the way, Zac has a new slogan. He ends each service with the admonition, "Do everything for the Kingdom."

It is only God and His kingdom upon this earth that can truly set men and women free.

Steve Fox, Junji Ono, and Ralph Moore with Bridge members
(1991).

Corey and Lisa Grinder at home in Tokorozawa, Japan
(1992).

Sean Odani, who is pioneering a church in Yokohama (1992).

Recent church leaders at Hope Chapel Hermosa.
L-R: Barry Felis, Chris Cannon, Steve Bliss, Henry Kaney,
Zac Nazarian.

Zac preaching

Family Festival at Hope Chapel Hermosa

Hope Chapel Staff & Family 1985: Ralph, John Honold,
Aaron Suzuki, Steven Suzuki, Eric Suzuki, Richard Pettit,
Debra Tong, Carl Moore, Ruby Moore, Stephanie Suzuki,
Erin Suzuki, Bonnie Thomas, Kelly Moore, Susan Regalado.

Office Staff 1993: **Top Row**; Ralph Swan, Junji Ono, Ka'ala
Souza, Ron Chambers, Aaron Suzuki, Ralph Moore, Sonia
Hirata, Lisa Lum, Darin Chang, Mark Hsi **Middle Row**;
Gisele Ferreira, Glory Yoshida, Colleen Kalama, Shireen
Koki, Tisha Falcon, Debra Grant, Michele Marugame, Patty
Ching **Bottom Row**; Allan Lau, Daven Hee, Wendell
Elento, Robert McWilliams, James Tongg, John Honold

Pastor Sonny Shimaoka of Hope Chapel Kona, who pioneered the first daughter church in 1984.

Pastor John and his wife Brenda Honold pioneering the 30th church in Hawaii, Hope Chapel Kapolei, in 1993.

Aerial view of Hope Chapel Kaneohe future building site

View from our property overlooking Kaneohe Bay

AVAILABLE FROM
STRAIGHT STREET PUBLICATIONS

BK101 Choices by Ralph Moore $5.95
God's will for your life as you see the freedom He gives us
to make CHOICES.

BK102 Let Go Of The Ring by Ralph Moore $9.95
Experience the life-giving principle of releasing power,
position and control and how it affects the growth of a
church.

BK103 Financial Freedom by Ralph Moore $7.95
By following biblical guidelines, you can learn to control
your finances instead of letting your finances control you.
This is a great tool to help the Pastor in his approach to
teach people to tithe.

WM101 Carry Me Away $8.00
Contemporary praise and worship songs that have become
standard favorites at Hope Chapel Kaneohe.

WM102 Hearts On Fire $8.00
First in a series of albums featuring the songs of various
artists from Hope.

WM103 I Will Sing Your Praise $10.00
This is Hope Chapel's first recorded "live" album. It
captures an evening of praise and worship.

WM104 In The Strength Of Your Love
                    Cassette $10.00   CD $15.00
Recorded two years after I Will Sing Your Praise, this is
Hope Chapel Kaneohe's newest praise and worship tape.

ORDER
FORM

FOR

STRAIGHT STREET
PUBLICATIONS
P. O. BOX 608
KANEOHE, HI 96744
(808) 235-5814
FAX (808) 247-2070

SHIP TO: DATE_____

NAME _____

ORGANIZATION_____

ADDRESS_____

CITY_____ STATE _____ ZIP _____

TELEPHONE (_____)_____

Quantity	Order Code	Description & Title	Unit Price	Total Price

METHOD OF PAYMENT (CIRCLE ONE) Check Money Order Master Card / VISA	Subtotal	
Please make check or money order payable to **STRAIGHT STREET PUBLICATIONS**	Postage & Handling *See Below	
Credit Card #	**Total**	
Signature Expiration Date	Postage & Handling If your total is Up to $20, add $2.00 $20 - $50, add $4.00 Over $50, add 8%	